I0527916

# HOLDING ON AND LETTING GO
## (IN) GOLF & LIFE

Michael J. Young, M.D. and John L. Perri, M.D.

*Dedicated to everyone who plays in the game—of life.*

## Also, by Michael J. Young, M.D.

*The Illness of Medicine (non-fiction)*

*Consequence of Murder*

*Net of Deception*

*To Cure or Kill*

# Table of Contents

# Introduction

There are bookshelves in libraries and bookstores lined with thousands upon thousands of titles describing "how to." These are publications whose authors are attempting to give the reader guidance and instruction on topics that vary from how to make do with what you have to how to perform (fill-in-the-blank) at the highest level. These books share the pearls of wisdom experienced by experts who try to help you with their vast knowledge and understanding. Whatever topic you are investigating, there is most likely a how-to book on those shelves–including many on the game of golf. There are also tens if not hundreds-of-thousands of additional magazine and journal articles written over many years by professional golfers and instructors about the game of golf. These, too, are written with the intent of helping the aspiring golfer learn techniques to practice the game and, hopefully, play better.

Perhaps it's best to provide you with a disclaimer about what you are about to read: this is not one of those books. We are not golf instructors, nor do we claim to have even a modicum of golf-teaching expertise–that will be left up to the true professionals who have a thorough understanding of golf swing mechanics. We are not physicists, aeronautical engineers, or mathematicians who can explain the nuances of golf ball flight, rotational spin, and motion. Indeed, in this book, neither one of us professes to understand how to teach the game most effectively. But that is not the point. We are obviously not golf professionals, and like so many others who love the game, we struggle with the game of golf–both the physical and mental aspects of the game.

Perhaps the question you should ask yourself is what in the world does a urologist and a psychiatrist know about the game of golf, and, secondly, how can reading this treatise help me? The answer is quite simple: we know little about *teaching* golf, but reading what we have to say might enlighten or facilitate your *realization* of certain aspects of the game.

You see, acquiring *knowledge* and having an *understanding* of that knowledge are intimately related, yet they represent totally separate proficiencies. As noted, we have a limited amount of knowledge about the mechanics of the golf swing. We know the things we have gleaned from years of taking lessons, watching television and videos, and reading publications. And, we understand a great deal about the game. However, knowledge of facts versus understanding how, when, and why to *apply* those facts to perform a particular activity is vastly different. We intend to extrapolate those understandings to a broader level of application. Most importantly, we hope to demonstrate that we understand a great deal about those who *play* the game.

It has been stated that golf is a microcosm of life. It is a frustration, and it is a joy. The game of golf can be your nemesis or your friend. On some days, you love it; on others, you want absolutely nothing to do with it. But golf is so much more than just a game to be played as a pastime or even as a professional sport. And, as we hope to demonstrate in this book, the game is not just a challenging activity to occupy the time. Rather, golf is a *revealer*. The game of golf reveals who the player is, who he or she aspires to be, and how they plan to achieve their goals. The question you need to now ask is, which game are we talking about? Is this a book about the game of golf, or is it about the game of life? In many ways, we hope to show you they are one and the same.

The modern game of golf has been around for a very long time. To our best understanding, it evolved in Scotland sometime in the 15th century. Over the centuries of playing this game, its rules and equipment have changed. A game that used to be played with a carved wooden club is now performed using scientifically designed steel and graphite shafts–the details of which are proprietary secrets and are, undoubtedly, incredibly complicated. Golf club heads are now designed and manufactured out of titanium and forged steel with the precision of a surgical instrument. Golf balls were originally made of wood. Later they were created by stuffing wet feathers into pockets formed from sewn leather strips (Feathery balls). Later, the dried sap of the Sapodilla tree was formed into ball shapes (Gutty balls). Rubber was the next material used. Today, golf balls are made by incorporating laboratory-produced, synthetic polymers that are extraordinarily consistent in how they play. The only significant variable in the game that *hasn't* changed since golf was invented is the human being holding the newfangled stick, striking the newly constructed ball with the titanium-headed club. The emotions, expectations, and behavior of the modern player are no different than those of his or her medieval counterpart.

We were all born some 600 years after the original golfers started smacking a ball around in a field with a simple club–but we *behave* similarly. And even though golfers through the years have witnessed countless societal, technological, and industrial advancements, we are still made up of the same DNA as the fellows who played with wooden balls and clubs. We have the same cognitive abilities and physical attributes as golfers from the Middle Ages. And, unfortunately, we share the same flaws— both mentally and physically, as our long-passed ancestors.

The authors are not golf experts. We are, however, keen observers of what motivates people to perform the way they do. We invite you to read our observations as we describe not how the game of golf is *played* but rather how we–players of golf, *think about playing* the game.

This is not a self-help book about golf. This is a self-*reflective* book about the game of golf and, importantly, the more significant games we play in our lives. We have learned the former is reflective of the latter. We are hopeful our insights and observations will enlighten you to perspectives that will assist you in both.

# Part I
# The Fundamentals: History and Basic Components of the Game

# Chapter 1
## *The Game*

The objective of this book is not to instruct anyone how to play the game of golf. As described, we are not qualified to do so. However, by using golf as a metaphor, we seek to analyze the game and its players as a means of examining how individuals navigate their worlds–their successes, failures, and the underlying motivations driving their behavior. We also wish to explore possible reasons a person accomplishes their goals–or fails in this task, by getting in their own way. Golf as an activity, as a game, and as a form of competition, appears perfect for this analysis. The game of golf simply doesn't deceive; rather, it reveals truths about the players and their approach to challenges.

Golf is one of the most intriguing activities to study. The ancient game started somewhere between Cro-Magnon Man roaming the earth with a real club and the advent of people riding bicycles. It is a ripe venue to discuss and review how we accomplish our goals–or don't. It is also a perfect study of how we interact (or play) with others and deal with adversity or good fortune.

For those unfamiliar with the game, watching televised tournaments provides a glimpse into its dynamics. The game's prime objective is for a player, using a club, to hit a small ball into a small cup at the end of a long stretch of grass using the fewest number of ball strikes (also called strokes). We will go into a more detailed description of the game and its rules for the non-golfers who may be reading this. But what you need to understand upfront is that the game is truly much more than just that.

For the uninitiated, golf is one of the few sporting endeavors played by an individual who is really competing against him or herself. Yes, there are competitors out on the course at the same time, but each player is really trying to play their best against the course. In other words, how I hit my golf shot does not impact how another player hits his or hers. We each play using our own ball and try to get the ball into the hole with the fewest number of strokes. How well I manage myself in performing this task on the course impacts only my score--not my playing companion. That is unless my playing companion (or competitor in a tournament) changes their game in response to my scoring. As you can see, it's an individual sport, but one's playing abilities or fortune can influence anyone else playing at the same time–quite an interesting dynamic. Similar to the 'real' world where our actions impact others, golf reflects this interconnectedness, highlighting how our individual choices reverberate within the broader context of the game–intended or not.

Let's start our exploration of golf by describing the game, its rules, and the objectives players aim to achieve. We understand that many readers may not have a complete grasp of golf's intricacies–from its rules and equipment to its playing etiquette and procedures. All of us know someone who plays the game; that individual is typically someone that, perhaps, we marvel at their dedication or, more commonly, we pity their addiction. We listen to their stories of glory, and we frown and do our best to console them when their day on the links isn't very kind. So, what's behind the enduring appeal of a 600-year-old game that can reduce a grown man to his knees over hitting a small ball into a hole? What is it about this game that exerts such control over its players? Why do otherwise rational individuals willingly endure adverse conditions like rain, mud, and strong winds – even snow – all in the name of golf? To play before dawn and well into the darkness–what is this game all about anyway?

In essence, golf is straightforward: Use a club – consisting of a grip, shaft, and head – to strike a ball as few times as possible into a predetermined hole in the ground. The modern game is played on a course (sometimes referred to as 'links') with the golfer attempting to get the ball into different designated holes–18

3

times. * At the conclusion of the 18 holes played, the player who has the fewest strokes is the winner. Golf holes can stretch longer than 700 yards in length, with some modern courses exceeding lengths of 8000 yards. Over centuries of play, every possible outcome of a golf shot has been meticulously accounted for. All possible results of striking a round object that flies then lands and rolls on an undulating, living surface have been defined by a multitude of rules adopted to play the game of golf. There are no deviations from the rules. We must be absolutely clear on this point: There are no deviations. Period. Full Stop. Well, no official deviations are permitted. We will discuss various player interpretations of the rules later.

Each hole is located on a specified area known as the 'green.' Perhaps this name was acquired because most of an ancient golf 'course' was un-watered fescue and dirt, and the 'green' was a gardened and tendered area. The area from where play begins (the tee box) to the green is called the fairway. As one begins to play from the tee box towards the green, the selection of clubs used will vary from those designed for maximum distance to those with maximum accuracy. (We will go into more golf club descriptions and details later). Once upon the green, the golfer will use what is referred to as a putter–because he or she is putting (or rather, rolling the ball) towards the hole. This club has a flat face and is occasionally referred to as the flat stick (because it is flat).

Sometimes, there are particularly challenging areas to play the ball between the tee box and the green. These areas may be hardened dirt, sand, tall grass, etc. The ball may still be playable, but to advance it towards the green will require additional skills. There are also areas where a player may hit his or her ball, so the ball may be lost or unable to be played. Areas where a player incurs penalties for hitting into are marked by specific lines and known as penalty areas. Examples of penalty areas may include ponds, lakes, or even the ocean. Hitting one's golf ball into the water may result in an impossible shot to get it out. Instead of trying to hit the ball from under the water, the player can accept a penalty stroke (an additional stroke added to his or her score) to allow the continuation of play. There are subcategories of rules for each of these circumstances. As stated earlier, the game is comprised of rules for the rules. The online version of the USGA Rules of Golf book is 162 pages in length! Let's just say we're covering the very basics.

All holes played will have boundaries, and the player must stay within those boundaries, or he or she will be penalized with additional stroke(s). Depending upon the local rules of a particular course (in addition to the standard rules already in place), a player may have to re-tee or 'drop' a ball in a specified area. There are no gray areas as to how the game is played.

As described, this game between gladiator-like competitors is won by determining which golfer, at the end of a 'round,' or 18 holes, has taken the fewest number of cumulative swings to advance the ball from each teeing area into the corresponding hole (also referred to as a cup) on each green. And, as would be expected in a game of detail, there are names for how many strokes one takes on each hole. If the golfer can get the ball into the hole in the 'expected' number of shots for a skilled** player, one is said to have made par. Who and how the number of expected strokes is determined is often something of a debate among those playing the game–particularly when the hole being played seems excessively long for the number of allocated strokes to make par. If a golfer is skilled (or lucky) enough to get the ball into the hole in one shot under par, he or she is said to have made a birdie. Birdies are a rare breed and are coveted. If the player is exceptionally good (and lucky!) and is able to sink the ball two strokes under par, the player will have bragging rights to say they shot an eagle. Eagles are as rare on the golf course as they are in the sky. For instance, an eagle on a par three-hole would also be called a hole-in-one. These are not only exceptionally rare, but they can also be expensive–the jubilant player is now responsible for all the drinks in the club bar following the round. (For unknown reasons, at some clubs, the hole-in-one-shooter must also purchase golf shoes for his or her foursome of players). On the other end of the playing spectrum, a player who holes out one shot over par is said to have scored a bogey. Two-shots-over-par is a double bogey. Three-shots-over-par is referred to as a triple bogey. Any more shots than that, and well, we understand it to be playing shitty golf. Best not to call it anything and just move on.

The choices regarding what equipment a player may use are purely in the hands of the golfer. Although the clubs and balls the player chooses must conform to defined standards (note the above discussion regarding the absolute rules of golf), the golfer is able to select equipment from a myriad of companies that produce his or her weapons of choice. The player chooses which brand of ball to play (less expensive is probably the wiser choice). He or she chooses which brand of golf clubs to use. The player can decide how long of a club to use, how heavy or light it is, and how flexible it is. And, of course, all these dimensions and variables must be within specified limits and of approved materials.

So, the golf ball sits on the grass unmoving until the golfer strikes it with his or her chosen club. It is completely up to the golfer to choose how and when he or she physically strikes the ball (but within 40 seconds of the time the player approaches the ball–as stated in the rules). Given that the golfer's swing is really the only thing moving (until the ball is struck), the game almost sounds too easy.

One must simply strike the small round ball that is sitting unmoving on the grass. Is it really that difficult? YES.

Despite the apparent advantages, how can a game that offers choice in equipment and ball, and involves hitting a stationary target, lead to such frustration and agony? Given the appearance of simplicity–hitting a stationary ball onto a large fairway of grass, how can this be so difficult? Many of these struck balls will end up lost in the woods, the neighboring home's lawn or windows, or at the bottom of a small pond. And, despite the enormous expense, time-consuming practice, and effort required to play a round that consumes most of the sunlit part of the day, many of us continue to go at it. So, what makes hitting the ball properly so challenging?

To understand the mechanics of hitting a golf ball, let's start with an introduction to the key anatomical component involved in the striking motion: the human brain. The human brain is made up of approximately 85-100 billion neurons (85,000,000,000–100,000,000,000). In addition, some 100 trillion synapses or connections whereupon messages can be sent or interrupted between these cells exist. A review of the unimaginable complexity of this organ is far beyond the scope of this review. However, in a somewhat watered-down explanation of this extraordinary organ, we can discuss a few key points.

The control of movement in humans depends on the activity and coordination of many aspects of our neuromuscular system. However, three separate but intertwined motor systems of the brain and the spinal cord are primarily engaged to accomplish muscular control. First, the corticospinal tract directs movement. It is the major neuronal pathway providing voluntary motor function. The corticospinal tract carries messages from the cortex of our brain to the motor neurons. Motor neurons comprise tightly controlled, complex circuits throughout the body that allow for voluntary and involuntary movements through the innervation of effector muscles and glands. Simplified, the corticospinal tract transmits instructions from our brain to our body when to perform a specific movement and precisely what to do to carry out that task: take a step, lift the leg, bend both the hip and the knee, etc. The second motor system that must engage in all purposeful movements is the cerebellar system. This system does not function consciously. The cerebellar system coordinates precise muscle movements necessary for executing actions and maintaining posture. The cerebellar system balances the degree of stimulation and relaxation of all the muscles that must contract and relax in order to carry out the orders relayed by the cerebral cortex to the designated muscular movements. Finally (and in vastly simple terms), the third motor system, the extrapyramidal system, is necessary to create and maintain posture. In order to swing a golf club successfully and hit the ball, the posture of the body must be rigorously controlled. No matter what the activity, all three systems must participate. [1]

But the difficulty in properly striking the golf ball goes well beyond our neuroanatomy and physiology. Hitting a round ball is never simple, no matter what the size of the ball or the shape of the club. As an illustration of basic physics, to increase the distance of a shot, golfers typically use longer clubs. As long as the swing remains constant, the radius of the arc increases in direct proportion to the length of the club. That increase in the distance traveled by the head of the club increases the speed of the head of the club. The increased speed of the head imparts greater force to the ball. The ball, having been hit with a greater force, travels farther. But wait, there is more. The weight of the head of the club must be considered. More weight means greater mass. Greater mass means more force. Greater mass results in a higher moment of inertia for the clubhead.*** This is not a simple direct product but one related to the fifth power of distance. Increased resistance to the fifth power of the distance

---

1 From: Why Michael Couldn't Hit, Harold L. Klawans,1996, W.H. Freeman

10

translates into a swing that is harder to initiate, harder to control, and far less reliable. Between a watered-down description of the complexities of our own anatomy, as well as just a superficial assessment of the rudimentary Newtonian physics involved in a club striking an object, one thing is for certain: golf is hard. In summary, the act of hitting a golf ball – aligning with the brain's desires, executing through neuromuscular anatomy, and adhering to the laws of physics – is a remarkable feat in itself.

To play the game with a modicum of success demands repeated rehearsals of a sequence of physical movements and 'ingraining' this activity into neural pathways so that when performed in a golf round, the movement is consistent and reliable. Generally speaking, this rehearsed movement doesn't change swing after swing. We've all practiced many things, and generally, with time, some success is achieved–or we quit and move on. But not the golfer. Nope. The golfer is a different breed of Homo sapiens. He or she will immerse themselves in expensive equipment, costly lessons, golf shoes, apparel, gloves, and, of course, hundreds (or maybe thousands) of balls. They will spend countless hours practicing the golf swing, thinking about the golf swing, and going over the details of their swing while at work and while participating in other life activities. It is all consumptive. Moving forward, let's delve deeper into the game of golf by exploring the equipment essential for gameplay.

## *The golf ball:*

As with most anything devised by compulsive reasoning and behavior, the dimensions of the golf ball are precise (recall the description of the rules): The ball is exactly 1.680 inches in diameter. Seriously. It has a circumference of 5.28 inches and a mass of 1.62 oz. To improve the golf ball's lift, or its ability to ascend after being struck, it features a unique attribute setting it apart from, for instance, a ping pong ball: dimples. Dimples are the little indentations seen on the ball–and there are lots of them. There are between 300 and 500 dimples on a modern golf ball with an average depth of about 0.010 inches. The indentations on the surface of the golf ball are there for a precise reason: they create airflow turbulence. Early golfers learned that the more nicks and scrapes on their Gutty golf balls, the higher the flight in the air compared to smooth balls. Air exerts a force on any object moving through it. Aerodynamicists break down the force into two components: lift and drag. Let's not delve into the complex mathematics of ball flight physics, but acknowledge that the dimples on a golf ball optimize lift force and minimize drag. Keep in mind, the choice of ball lies with the golfer. He or she may select to play a ball with more or fewer dimples, or a ball that is designed with a particular pattern of dimples that aeronautical engineers have ingeniously designed to create the ball flight a player desires. Understand many players are happy to simply hit the ball into the air, let alone concern themselves with how it flies! Such nuances of controlling ball flight are best left up to scratch golfers and professionals. (We will describe what a scratch golfer is and handicapping in another chapter). But for now, simply understand there are myriad golf ball options available. Currently, on the market, the modern-day golfer can select from multiple brands and types of golf balls. Major manufacturers offer various ball types tailored to different skill levels and abilities. Balls may be claimed to offer high flight, reduced spin, increased distance, or improved feel. Whatever ball characteristics a player is looking for can be found in the modern golf ball. There is also a rainbow of colors of golf balls available to aid those who have difficulty seeing their balls in the air after their flailing swing. Perhaps they have trouble seeing it because the recently struck ball is just dribbling on the ground. Other than the potential visual enhancement of brightly colored golf balls, I suspect some of the variety of available color options are really just for fun. But I digress–choose whatever brand, color, dimple pattern, or box cover you like. Give a pro any ball, and he or she will hit it high and far.

*Golf clubs:*

We should now spend some time examining the modern golf club. After all, the game is played by striking the non-moving, dimpled, 1.62 oz object sitting on the grass with the club. I suspect most of us have been hitting things ever since some of us realized at a young age we have a sibling for practice. I'm also quite sure some of us also learned to do this quite well. The days of the 'ancient' clubmaker pounding away in his small shop are long gone. The process of putting together a club today relies on data gleaned from sophisticated computer programs and monitors designed to measure every nuance of the player's swing. The modern club has certainly advanced from the Days of Thor. No longer made of a hickory wooded shaft and an iron head, the current golf club is constructed of a variety of materials and composites. Modern shafts are made of graphite, steel, or a combination of both materials. The complexity of how the laminate construction of the various club shafts is now made is akin to building a rocket. Designing and constructing club shafts is a highly specialized field, with manufacturers closely guarding their proprietary materials and processes. The head of the modern club is made of ceramic, steel, titanium, or any number of alien materials forged together to create something that deserves a more sophisticated purpose than striking a little ball on grass. Today, the modern golfer is also no longer hindered by a simple leather grip to hold onto the club. Every golfer now has dozens of different grips to choose from. The modern golf grips–designed with mathematical consideration and a precise understanding of the golfer's hand and fingers are remarkable. Using new-age rubber or similarly modified materials, the grips' varying locations of flexibility and firmness, all scientifically designed to improve how one grabs and holds onto the club, have brought the experience of holding a club to another level.

One of the most important aspects to understand about the golf club is the angle of the face of the club. This is also known as the *loft*. As each player decides which clubs he or she wishes to use, every player can select how much loft or angle he or she wishes to use to hit the ball. A more open-angled club face will cause the ball to ascend higher in the air, while a more vertical face on the club will cause the impacted ball to fly lower and typically farther. For those wondering, that is why a golfer carries a variety of clubs in their bag. The player is carrying clubs with different club face lofts and shaft lengths to allow the player to adjust how high and far they hit each ball. But here's the rub: The golfer is allowed to carry only 14 clubs in his or her bag for a round of golf. This rule of limiting one's arsenal of equipment makes the game so much more interesting and challenging. However, there are two clubs that make up part of the 14 and are responsible for more agony for the golfer than the other 12 clubs combined. Those clubs–the putter and the driver, must be discussed in further detail.

### *The Putter:*

The putter is arguably the most personal and intimate of all the clubs in one's bag. It is chosen by the golfer by selecting it from literally hundreds of other models–all designed to do one thing: to roll the ball on the green into the hole. As discussed previously, the object of the game is for the golfer to get the ball into the hole on the green in as few strokes as possible. Once a player has reached the green with the array of clubs in their arsenal, he or she must now get the damn ball into the hole. The club to best accomplish this task is the putter. The ball is 'putt' or rolled into the hole–again noting that each putt is considered a stroke and counts just as much as a 300-yard drive. A particular brand or type of putter is chosen for any number of reasons–its look, its feel, the quality of its advertisement, its cost, and most importantly, its ability to work in the store just prior to purchase.

For reasons that have baffled golfers for probably centuries, once that special putter is selected and paid for, it will do any number of unexplainable things–like become 'cold' and fail to work as expected. Most non-organic objects in the world are at the same temperature as the ambient or surrounding environment. Putters are different. These unique objects have been found by scientists to do something most unusual: They can become 'hot' or 'cold.' In my experience, they mostly become cold, even on the hottest of days. Simply put, the putter is the golfer's best friend or his worst enemy. Golfers typically have a garage or closet full of previously purchased putters (some priced upwards of $500) that have somehow let their owner down or have lost their once-perceived magic. The putter must be able to sink putts consistently and reliably–from long distances on the green to the knee-knocking 2-footers. Depending upon the day, the weather forecast, and probably most importantly, the alignment of Jupiter and Mars, a putter can be magical and sink every putt or be unable to do anything as desired. The putter is a very mysterious club. It must be handled with the utmost care and spoken to with kind words of encouragement before each use. Its failure to produce desired outcomes leads to misbehavior, uncontrollable outrage, and, most likely, excessive drinking during and after the round. But again, as with everything else used in the game, the golfer chooses his putter. Choose wisely, friend.

### *The Driver:*

The driver is another story altogether–by far, it is the sexiest club in our bag. It is the beast, the dog, the big stick–it is designed to hit the ball off the tee the farthest with the loudest sound and fury. Although it is affectionately referred to as a wood (because the clubhead of drivers for many years was made of hardened wood), a modern driver is so much more than that. Indeed, the modern driver is composed of materials of space-age complex combinations, and even manufacturers haven't been able to give them flattering names. Commonly available drivers have names like Epic, Rogue, Stealth, Paradym and Launcher. They are given numbers and insignias, much like a military machine. Drivers are big, shiny monsters advertised to hit the ball into infinity. The new drivers are made of steel, ceramic, titanium, probably a bit of plutonium, and perhaps a touch of mercury. It is known among golfers that a ball that is driven well (long and straight down the middle of the fairway) can intimidate opponents and give the golfer a sense of strength and power. However, as with most uses of power, if uncontrolled, it can lead to absolute mayhem and misery. A poorly driven tee shot (one that is perhaps hit far but way offline) can suck the energy out of a golfer in an instant. The bravado that was initially felt as the Excalibur of drivers is removed from the golf bag and set up to the ball, can disappear in a flash.

No matter how well a golfer plays a hole–perhaps making par or even a birdie, his next shot will undoubtedly employ the driver, and all bets are off: We all hold our collective breaths as the proud and sturdy golfer stands on the tee box and unloads his big dog on the little, dimpled ball. We all wait and watch with excited anticipation as the golfer swings the mighty driver. We hear the '*crack*' of the clubface impaled at supersonic speeds into the side of the ball. So often, it's just a teaser–the ball goes dribbling off the tee, is topped and rolls a few dozen yards, or it screams to the far right or left. Sometimes, when the ball is given a mighty blow from a poorly swung drive, the ball is never to be located again–it is lost in the woods, the tall grass, or perhaps it has found a watery grave. The mystery of properly hitting the driver is a challenge all golfers try to achieve. Few of us ever master the driver, but oh, how we love to hit it! As with all the other clubs in the bag, we choose our drivers. We choose our beasts for the tee box.

## *Golf Shoes:*

Golf shoes are an interesting and necessary piece of equipment to play golf well. They are designed to hold our feet in place and not twist in the grass as we unload vast amounts of power and torque during the swing. The shoe is often overlooked as an importnt part of our ability to strike the ball well. Perhaps more important than its function on the grass is how it looks. Any devoted, addicted golfer must have a vast selection of golf shoes. For women, the rules surrounding the golf shoe of choice can be overwhelming. Their shoes must not only function to keep their feet securely on the ground, but the shoes must match their golf outfits–It's a mandatory rule at most clubs. Men are the same–they just pretend it's not as important.

So, there it is. The basics of the game, the equipment, the apparel, the balls–all the key components one needs to play the game of golf. Of course, we have ignored the time it takes to play, to prepare...and to shop. The time to exercise and stretch, the time set aside for lessons (and the work we must do to pay for those lessons). The last remaining piece of equipment that seems to be the most difficult to master and the most challenging to understand is the mind of the golfer.

What we are referring to as the mind of the golfer goes beyond neuroanatomical structure and stimulus-response patterns. We are talking about symbolic reasoning, a capacity unique to humans. In other words, we don't operate in the world based solely on instincts. Unlike other species, we possess a built-in, hard-wired, self-reflective faculty that is constantly active, for better or for worse. We are constantly evaluating our experiences, attaching symbolic meanings, which then have emotional, even spiritual reverberations. We have a constant internal dialogue that accompanies our self-awareness, sometimes acting as a supportive ally and at other times as a formidable adversary. This internal commentary is nearly a continuous companion to our understanding of self. The experience of the golfer is the same. However, in the realm of golf, emotional moments often become amplified. We have all seen this, and most of us have experienced it.

Who can forget Jean van de Velde's epic collapse in the 1999 British Open at Carnoustie Golf Links? It was absolutely agonizing to watch. For those readers who are unfamiliar with this event, those of us watching observed a golfer leading arguably the most prestigious golf tournament in the world–up to and including the very last hole. Van de Velde appeared to suffer from a combination of poor judgment, subpar performance, and unfortunate luck, resulting in his loss of the tournament, televised worldwide. Even after 25 years, it remains a tragic event etched in memory. Yes, it was only golf. But you must stand in awe of the emotional power this game can unleash. Jean van de Velde survived the event, but the scars for all who watched remain. To grasp the gravity of this event, a quick web search of his name will reveal numerous articles and commentaries detailing that fateful day at Carnoustie. There was even a full-length documentary released in 2018 detailing the tournament. So, what do we make of all this? And perhaps more importantly, what do we do with it? In the chapters ahead, we aim to provide insights into these complex questions: what drives golfers' behavior, and more broadly, what parallels can be drawn to human behavior?

*Why 18 holes are played in a 'round' of golf has been debated for centuries. Some have speculated those who 'invented' the game simply quit after 18 holes. Historians have surmised the game originally had more holes, but then in 1764 at The Old Course at St. Andrews in Scotland, four short holes were combined into two (and played in two directions). Other courses followed suit or made modifications of their own. Urban legend notes that a bottle of whisky has 18 shots in it–go figure.

**The definition of a skilled player is somewhat subjective. The term 'par' in golf comes from the stock exchange term meaning "equal."

***You had to ask. In simplified terms, the moment of inertia (MOI) is defined as the quantity expressed by the body resisting angular acceleration, which is the sum of the product of the mass of every particle with its square of the distance from the axis of rotation.

# Chapter 2
## *Before We Go Any Further...*

Before we go any further, we need to spend a little time on how golfers assess their abilities in the game of golf. As described previously, hitting a golf ball is a complicated integration of body movement, relying significantly on coordination and synchronization. But simply performing these complex events is not enough to make a hard game even harder. As humans roam the earth, they have a constant need to know how they relate to others. They wonder if their skills are comparable to those of others who are attempting the same tasks. Perhaps this dates back to The Days of Thor, as he needed to know his hunting prowess was better than everyone else's. If everybody failed to hit a small ball in the direction and with the distance desired, then we would all feel better about our inability to do so. But, as with most everything in life, some will do it better. In fact, some will do it so well that trying to play against them would simply be a waste of time and effort. The Days of Thor— comparing who is stronger, faster, or 'better' must be part of our primal brain. Consequently, an equitable (albeit sometimes challenging to understand) system was devised to allow golfers to compare and compete against one another. It is referred to as the Handicap System.

Golfers sitting around the clubhouse remind me of the old EF Hutton television commercials. As a result of several mergers in the 1990s, the original EF Hutton eventually became part of Citigroup and later Morgan Stanley Wealth Management, a joint venture between Morgan Stanley and Citigroup. The original EF Hutton commercials are tremendously apropos. In those commercials, a person is seen quoting his or her investment advisor, who happens to work for EF Hutton. The investor speaking would quietly and confidently announce to someone sitting next to him what the EF Hutton advisor suggested for a stock investment. Suddenly, everyone in the room quiets down to carefully listen to the whispered recommendation. In a similar way, competitive golfers are interested in the capabilities of their fellow club members. (Think Thor).

A golf handicap index is a numerical measure of a golfer's ability, or potential ability, used to enable players of different skill levels to compete against one another. In the past, golfers could only learn about others' handicaps through direct communication or via tournament and club committees. It would be a great curiosity to know others' indexes. Only through whispered discussions in the members' lounge would club members learn the precious handicap of those who shared the same locker room and facilities. Today, we live in a world where much of our lives are stored in accessible databases and within every looming 'cloud.' And, like everything else, there is a means to access that data. Through a variety of websites and Apps, the handicap of all players who play the game competitively can be found without so much as leaving your favorite chair with a smartphone in hand. Make a few clicks, and a player can see the handicap of any player in the country. What a wonderful time to be a golfer. Golf handicaps are a calculated number that represents a golfer's ability based on their previous golf round scores. The better the player, the fewer strokes he or she is handicapped for competitive play. No doubt, this calculation is performed by a massive supercomputer located in a secret location deep in a national security facility. In a nutshell, the lower your golf handicap index, the more skilled you are in the game. When competing against a player with a higher handicap, the more shots (strokes) the skilled player must 'give' the lesser skilled player to compete equitably. The system aims to enable players of varying skill levels to compete fairly in a given round or tournament, determining the better player at that specific moment. The actual mathematical algorithm used to calculate the index can get rather complicated. Factors that are integrated into these advanced mathematical calculations include the degree of difficulty of the courses played and the length of the courses. At times, the methodology appears to incorporate factors like humidity, pollen count, lunar positioning, and other variables, which can seem rather mysterious. In all honesty, very few players truly understand how a handicap is determined. Given the handicap will vary depending upon each score entered, the number can change with each round of golf. Competitive golfers know their own (and their friends') handicap like a dog knows where it buried its last bone.

As we proceed in our discussion of the golf game, reference will be made frequently to the handicap. It's an important number that players use to compare themselves to others. However, this calculated assessment of their playing ability will also allow the player to know how he or she is playing comparatively to themselves at different points in time. For instance, a player may be taking a series of golf lessons and want to know if their game is improving. Utilizing scores from various courses and different levels of difficulty provides an objective measure for personal assessment. Without applying handicap indexing, it's difficult to make a fair comparison of play based solely on scores.

So now, we hopefully understand the objectives of the game. We understand what is involved in physically hitting the golf ball, and we know how to assess how we are doing in that effort. It's time to delve into the most challenging aspect of the game of golf–understanding the golfer. Through this evaluation and discussion, we aim to gain insights into what drives us on and off the course.

# Chapter 3
## *Games People Play*

***The Gimme:***

We all love gimmes. Gimmes are the freebies in life that just make our day. Gimmes make us feel good, as we don't have to do anything for them–except be there with an open hand and accept them as they roll into our little worlds. The gimmes in life are our reward for being around at just the right time and place. Or, perhaps, gimmes are better explained as being around the right people at the right time and place. Gimmes are what we hope for when the stress is on. They keep us going without a need to defend or explain ourselves. After all, "it was just given to me."

There are also gimmes in the game of golf...and believe it or not, they are unabashedly called 'gimmes.' A typical example of a gimme in golf is the conceded putt. For instance, let's say I'm playing a round of golf with some friends, and we're on the green waiting our turn to putt (the person farthest away from the hole putts first, and this continues until all the balls are holed). If the putt I have is short and likely easy to make, friends in a casual game often call it a "gimme," assuming you would sink it. They will tell you to simply pick up the ball without the requisite that you make the putt. They give it to you; it's a gimme. The friendlier the game (and one without any wager or betting), the longer the gimme distance becomes. In fact, refusing to grant gimmes for straightforward putts might earn you some unfriendly looks or comments from your playing partners. It's like failing to open the door for someone entering a door that you are exiting. Of course, you are expected to hold the door for them. But... some people don't.

Like everything in golf, there are rules. Sometimes, the rules are unwritten. Nonetheless, they are still the rules and must be followed. In tournament medal play, meaning you are participating in an event that counts each and every stroke made during the round, it is highly unlikely that your opponent will simply let you have a gimme. The stakes (mostly pride and bragging rights at the amateur level–but sometimes money as well) are on the line. However, on occasion, your opponent may decide to give you a short putt. But free isn't necessarily free. Don't think for a minute that the decision to give you that putt wasn't carefully considered as a strategic move on your opponent's part. They may be giving you the free putt because they expect you to return the favor later during the round. They may also be giving you the gimme, so you don't have a 'reason' to make the putt... meaning, if you don't take the putt, you similarly don't get a chance to feel the green speed or assess the slope. By not putting, you are sacrificing the experience of putting. If this strategy is applied early in the competition, it may cause you to lower your guard and actually putt worse. Later in the round, you may benefit from having more putting opportunities, and that early one given to you will leave you with one less opportunity to experience the break of the green. It's uncanny how calculating some players can be. So, remember, the free putt given to you isn't necessarily an act of kindness or good sportsmanship. For some, there are no gimmes in life, and everything is a competition. What appears to be a gimme is just a very subtle way for some to camouflage their real intent. So be careful of the freebies in the world–free isn't without a price.

## *You Go First*

Who doesn't like to go first? Going first is usually quite an honor. In fact, chivalry even demands that ladies go first. Isn't that the proper etiquette? Yes...sometimes. But going first can also lead to some untoward consequences. For instance, I can recall numerous times skiing on an unfamiliar mountain. It was always more prudent (and safe) to have the advantage of watching someone else go first so I could then assess the proper path or speed to take. Maybe I would even see the lead person fall. Then...maybe I'll take that into consideration and try an alternative route to the bottom. Not being first does have its advantages.

The tee box is an interesting area to go to first while playing golf. You see, other than the first hole, where the decision as to who goes first is determined by an arbitrary system (by draw), golf employs the honor system on all subsequent holes. The player who had the best score on the previous hole now has the honor of teeing off first. This is not necessarily as honorable as it may appear. In fact, I know some very clever players who somehow always find a way to tee off last–regardless of how they scored on the previous hole. Oh, they fiddle around, jiggle a few clubs, tie their shoes, or find any number of ways to simply not be ready to tee off when the group assembles on the tee box. And, as (most) everyone wants to get moving along in the round, the honor ends up going to whoever decides to stride up and plant their tee peg into the ground first. Sometimes, this can lead to seeing consequences that advantage the person teeing off second or third, or, as our constantly delayed friend seems to manage so often, last. Discovering the water hazard (pond or creek) as a factor only occurred when golfer number one sent their ball plunging into it. Or nobody could clearly see the sand trap was that close to the green–until player number one plops one in there. A more common finding is the effect of the wind, which nobody could appreciate before seeing a ball fly through it. Each subsequent player will learn a bit more about the fairway they now find themselves playing. So, going first isn't always the honor the rules of the game imply. Be mindful of playing partners (business, work, acquaintances) who like to always watch you take the first step. They will often benefit from your experiences.

## *Wagers and Bets*

Perhaps it's just a consequence of being part of a competition. I mean, at its core, golf is the player testing his or her wits and skills against nature and the golf course. It's the player's experience, athleticism, and knowledge of their capabilities that allows him or her to navigate the course they are playing. The player also matches his skills with the trickery and false enticements the course architect may have devised in order to confuse or cause the player to attempt shots that are unlikely to be successful. It's me against the course, and the course will always have subtleties and nuances that I may not be aware of until I've fallen victim to their presence. For instance, the back of the green has a steep slope (that I can't see from a distance), such that a ball hit too far will slide off and drop into a tiny little creek running behind the green. There might be a bunker that appears flat, yet once in it, the front lip is so high that it will take no less than three shots to get out. Unseen fairway moguls may exist, preventing the player from ever having a flat lie. There are numerous ways the course designer can build his layout to make the player suffer. It's his bet he can beat me, and it's my bet that I can take on whatever lies in front of me. And so, it's game on!

However, often I find myself in a four-ball round where everyone seems eager to engage in betting. A friend of mine once told me that "every golf shot makes someone happy." If I hit the ball well, I'm pleased. If I hit it poorly, my competitors (or even my 'friends') may have a hidden smirk behind their false statements of condolence. Sometimes, it's hard to determine who is with or against you. Indeed, golf mirrors life in many ways, as we've discussed before.

I will state from the get-go: I'm not a big gambler. People who play golf with me know I never initiate any betting, and I'm usually the last person they turn to as the decision of which betting game to play is discussed. But to be part of the group and not be the party pooper, I reluctantly join in.

There are golf betting games galore! Practically every time I play with a new group of golfers, I'm introduced to another betting game, a variation of a game, or some other oddly concocted means to add, subtract, or divide some aspect of my score, which is then translated into a monetary value. I often don't understand the games, how the calculations are made, or why some of the games are even played. But what I do know is that people like to bet against others. It must be related to some primal need that is ingrained in the innermost part of our brain that enticed Thor to make comparisons to his nearest adversaries. If you're familiar with handicapping, you'll understand how a player's handicap is crucial in on-course betting.

The player's handicap is the base number to which all other aspects of the betting games are based. For instance, if my handicap is 10, and yours is, say 20, it implies that I will shoot (about) 10 shots fewer than you on a given round. More accurately, the number of strokes used to calculate the differential is predicated on the actual course index–but let's not get too bogged down. Now, if a wager is placed based on that differential, you can see if I fail to beat you by that amount, I may have hell to pay...or at least some cash. This was an easy calculation. However, some games mandate an advanced mathematics degree from MIT to understand how the outcomes are determined. My experience has proven that, somehow, the person who introduces the game to the group seems to win the most. It's uncanny. And so, it goes–given the game's outcome is based on numbers (who wins and who loses), adding a wager to the mix is to be expected. Perhaps we love (or need) comparing ourselves to others. It validates our self-worth and gives us a slight endorphin rush when our worth is reaffirmed. Just take my money before we start; it alleviates all anxiety.

## *Keeping Up*

There are lots of ways to get into trouble on a golf course. Aside from hitting your ball out of bounds, losing a ball, plunking it into a water hazard, or breaking a neighbor's window, the game can be an absolute challenge filled with anxiety and emotion. One of the things that drives most players a bit crazy, however, has nothing to do with where their ball is hit. For some reason, we love to hate the group in front of us. You see, the game is typically played in groups of four players. Golf course management understands there is a certain level of time efficiency that needs to be maintained to keep all the groups on a course moving along. It's referred to as 'keeping pace.' Each course has determined a properly played round should take 'X' amount of time. The groups of players are expected to play within that allotted time and are often 'timed' by a course marshal. Timing can be measured, but more typically, how efficiently a group is moving is determined by how far back they are in relation to the group playing in front of them. If a group is falling back from the group in front, it will cause the entire course behind them to back up. If you thought a slow bumper-to-bumper day on the expressway was bad, it's far worse on the golf course. When we are supposed to be having fun, nobody wants to wait.

The dilemma that now occurs is what the group being held up does at this point. There are multiple options: do nothing and simply complain among playing peers, contact the clubhouse or flag down the course marshal to institute some encouragement for the slow pokes to move faster, or confront the slow players in front of you directly. I have seen all three play out. Rarely do any of them go well.

If your group is silently frustrated that the pace of play is equivalent to a herd of old goats crossing the street, everyone will only get more frustrated as the round proceeds. Frustration leads to a bad shot, which then leads to more frustration. This is usually contagious, and soon, the cycle repeats itself until everyone in the group is in a tense, frenzied state. At least everyone feels justified they now have an acceptable excuse for a shitty score. "Damn group in front of us was pitiful," is usually then heard in the members' lounge. A nod and a sigh of camaraderie is then shared by all. But there is also a communal sense of relief that we can all share our frustration together. The person I was most concerned with beating in my group is now my ally. The enemy of my enemy is my friend...or something like that.

To complain to the marshal, or worse yet, a cell phone call to the clubhouse, is a more advanced state of frustration. Typically, after such a call is made, the course marshal will come out and speak with the preceding group. Depending on how busy the day is (or how interested the marshal is), will determine if he shows up in 10 minutes or in 10 holes. When the marshal does show up to give a reprimand to the group in front for slow play, you're playing pals finally feel vindicated for the interminable wait they had to put up with. That's fine...up until the point when you see the marshal point in your group's direction. That's the clear sign those in front now know it was *you* who called the cops. Now, there may be hell to pay when you are done with your round.

I was once blamed by a club member for calling their group out for slow play. The angry member wouldn't speak or look at me for weeks. Finally, I approached him one day to discuss the issue. As it turned out, it was another player in my group who initiated the complaint, and this member mistakenly thought it was me. We were buds again. The lesson, I guess, is if you call out the group in front for slow play (equivalent to a felony charge), it's best to make it an anonymous call. It's also probably wise to know which marshal is on duty before making a complaint— some may shift blame. Perhaps an equivalent comparison could be when letting your landlord know about a noisy neighbor... remember to ask him not to reveal the source of the complaint.

And finally, we come to the most aggressive form of calling out the group in front of you for slow play. You actually...call them out. This has three outcomes–two of which are bad. In the best of all worlds, you ask them to move faster; they drop to their knees, beg for forgiveness, and apologize. They speed up immediately, and you feel like the star of your playing group. Considering the Days of Thor and typical male behavior, this outcome is highly unlikely. Unless all four members of the preceding group have been castrated, this is the rarest of outcomes.

The second outcome that occurs after you confront the group ahead is they appease you...and do nothing. Well, you tried. You were a gentleman, and they were cordial. As you walk or ride back to your awaiting group (who are standing there with bated breath), the group who gently said, "Yes, why of course we will speed up," now tell themselves that you can go fuck yourself. Well, no harm, no foul.

But the most dreaded outcome–which is always present in the back of your mind as you approach the slow group ahead, is they react with uncontrollable rage. Unkind words are shared with you, and actual threats of violence are just a few synapses away from happening. It's generally known that when an adversary (the group in front of you) starts to behave in a threatening manner, it's probably best to hightail it back to whence you came. Although the days of sword fighting are probably best remembered to have occurred in the Middle Ages (about the time when golf was invented), it's ironic a club drawn from a golf bag could be used in a similar fashion. When you voice your complaints, and the alpha male in the front group starts going to his bag to get his driver out, that's probably a good sign you've overstayed your welcome. Best to now say "thank you" and bid your adieu. Even though the knuckleheads are slow... and probably slightly inebriated, this is not the time to be Thor. Thor didn't live a long life.

We titled this chapter 'Games people play.' But do the preceding descriptions strike you as all fun and games? Hardly. In fact, each situation described has a dark side, i.e., a 'gimme' can easily morph into a harsh test of reciprocity, with potential animosity and grudges held depending on the goodwill expressed or withheld. Same with the 'honor system'. This system can be manipulated for a competitive advantage—a stark departure from the noble concept of 'honor.' Wagers and bets, pace of play–are these good-natured and playful parts of the game? To some extent, yes. We call it friendly competition. And for the most part, we participate as good sports. But let's be honest, golf is not a lighthearted romp in the meadow. No, it's akin to a demanding discipline, albeit one hopefully seasoned with camaraderie, allowing us to partake in those moments we all recognize as 'why we keep coming back.'

And come back, we do. Golf is a wonderfully unique game. There is always the hope that the next shot, the next round, the next season will be better. At times, this feels like an illusion. But it's also a tantalizing offer to 'get better,' perhaps even excel.

Ironically, having a more playful attitude can help us improve. It's when we start playing games in emotionally dishonest ways we get into ruts, and our game suffers.

So, play your best game and hope others play theirs as well.

# Chapter 4
## *The Social Context*

Having reviewed the fundamental rules and equipment used in the game, and before launching into a more detailed analysis of how we approach and deal with golf et al., perhaps a brief look at a few of the game's more subtle etiquette issues will be useful. Understand many of these concerns reach far beyond the confines of the fairways and greens.

As mentioned, golf reveals a person's character. How someone reacts to failure, reacts to success, handles disappointment, and interacts with fellow players or competitors can tell so very much about someone's personality. Thus, there are players I genuinely enjoy spending time with.

Then there are days when I'm stuck in an unfortunate 'pairing' that I'd rather be in a dental chair having a root canal performed by a proctologist. Sometimes in life, we don't get to choose how, when, and with whom we must spend our time. So, we grin and bear it. Perhaps it's best we all learn how to get inside a bubble now and then and focus on ourselves–sometimes, it's a matter of simple survival.

The Social Context

### *Music:*

The evolving use of music in golf is quite interesting. We live in a world that blasts us 24/7 with news, texts, and emails all day. Many people have difficulty taking vacations–real vacations, away from the constant bombardment of inclusion text threads and emails from work. Unless you refuse to turn on your phone, pad, or laptop computer while away, you are never separated from the constant influx of information streaming into your world. And, although you may feel you are simply 'checking in' when you quickly read the text thread or work email, the actual effects on you are much more significant than you realize. Once the data or information is 'input,' your mind will promptly begin disarticulating and analyzing whatever you just read or heard while simply checking in. Physically, you may close the computer or phone and then move to whatever is on your schedule, but your noggin will continue to process all the information and data it is exposed to–like it or not–that's what it does. Our brain never stops working–analyzing or integrating whatever it has been exposed to. How many times in your life have you been engaged in a particular activity–even sleeping, when an idea pops into your head? The brain continuously processes problems, questions, emotions, and details of our lives far beyond what we are cognitively aware of; the subconscious never turns off. Until we shut off the inflow of stimulation, the brain will continue to work on it. Personally, I find it takes me about three days of vacation time until I feel like I'm actually relaxing. It takes me that long to 'work out' whatever problems and issues I'm focused on before I'm able to unplug myself from my daily routine.

If you look around, you will see children glued to their iPads. You will notice adults tied to their computers, earbuds inputting music, sound, or conversation. Cellphones are carried tightly in hand as people cross the street–can't they let up for just a few moments to pay attention to the passing cars? Can't that next text or call wait even a few seconds or even a few minutes? Are people so addicted to these devices–so in need of constant stimulation they can't put them down for a moment? If people are constantly stimulated from the outside, perhaps they can't focus on what's being processed on the inside. The brain is trying to work on what was inputted moments ago, but new information is being added each awake moment! Maybe it's not a coincidence we see more and more individuals with attention disorders, sleep problems, weight issues, or anxiety. People just don't allow themselves time off. Or maybe they don't want to. Maybe the constant stimulation of music, news, conversation, and information are wanted distractions from allowing themselves to think. Thinking is hard–sometimes it's painful. Perhaps many would rather be engaged by this constant information input and not have to deal with their own thoughts.

Over the last decade, the development of portable Bluetooth speaker devices has crept its way into the quiet calm of the golf course. Speakers that clip onto a golf bag, are attached to golf carts, and even small speakers that attach to one's pocket are now commonplace out on the course. Really? Even on a golf course? Do golfers really need this constant bombardment from their favorite sounds to induce an improvement in their play? Perhaps time spent on the course is no different than their time everywhere else–a constant need for stimulation and less time to be confronted with their own contemplation. Some will say the music relaxes them–it helps them to focus. We can appreciate that perspective. Many of us listen to music while trying to unwind or, perhaps, to find motivation. But do we have to listen to your music when not interested in listening? Do we have to listen to what you have chosen as your inspirational songs?

Despite the human ego that proclaims what 'I' do is okay, it may come across as a shock, but other golfers may not like the type of music you listen to. Most golfers are considerate and don't want to make a fuss. They will nod their heads and agree that what you want to do is okay. But it isn't. Although no one may say anything as you play your rock, country music, or whatever it is you enjoy, we all cherish our space. Some of us want the quiet calm of a golf course to get away from the daily stimulation, noise, and chatter. So, if you must always be piped in for whatever your need or reason, do everyone else a favor. If you can't find a way to turn it off, then put in earbuds. Turning it down is not the same as turning it off. Nobody wants to hear you sing on the course, and they probably don't care to hear your music either–no matter how softly you play it. So be respectful of others who are sharing that moment on the course. Quiet doesn't happen too often in our world anymore, and you might use this opportunity for a period of self-reflection on what you are doing and why. Who knows, you might actually enjoy the experience.

## *Talking:*

There are those who like to talk, and talk, and talk...and there are definitely times in life when you need to speak. For instance, while in a theater where there is a fire, most people ask you to announce the emergency. If you strike a golf ball veering right at someone, I'm sure they would appreciate you yell "fore!" and inform them they may soon get beaned.

For most players, golf takes a considerable amount of their time–and it isn't just the actual playing time that needs to be considered. Getting to a club mandates significant planning and effort. Not only does it take time to get to the course and back, but it also means time doing other, perhaps even necessary activities, is put on hold or not done at all. We are each at the golf course because we choose to be. But on someone's backswing, they really don't need to know about your Aunt Tilda's health problems. Similarly, although it may be critically important to you, most of us don't want to hear a long, detailed description of your swing problems–doing so will make me lose focus, and your issues will soon become mine. We all made an effort, planned ahead, and most likely gave up something else in order to be on the course. This time is important. Respect the other golfers' time and let them enjoy their round as they wish. If they're up for conversation, they'll indicate so.

### *Excessively Slow Play:*

We all have days when our ability to focus is not at its best, and we have more indecision than usual. Similarly, we all have days when we are playing poorly and spend more time looking for balls in the fescue or helping our playing mates find theirs. But...that does not mean you have to spend 3 minutes on each putt, or plan and prepare each shot as though the Ryder Cup team score is dependent upon your play; we've got news: it isn't. And for the average player–which means most of us, you don't need to play from the tips. We can't count the number of times a testosterone-laden group of young studs decide they want to experience the whole course. Along with the accompanying excessive drinking, which slows them down more than they are aware, they have no business trying to replicate the tour pros. Honestly, despite your occasional great drive, you really don't belong in the back. Play to your abilities, try to keep up with the playing group in front of you, and, importantly, be respectful of those behind you.

### *Being a doctor to strangers*

As physicians, we're used to friends and acquaintances calling or asking for advice for a specific medical condition they or someone they know is experiencing. It's our pleasure to try to help them understand unclear terminology or an upcoming medical procedure. Nobody wants to be a patient and depend on another for treatment. It is a very unsettling situation. We're often asked for referrals or suggestions regarding medical issues, and we're always happy to assist. That's what friends are for.

However, it's surprising how many absolute strangers we meet on a golf course who feel their health issues are mandated to be our focus of attention while trying to play. Because we have expertise in something that is of concern, we should not be interrupted by their questions and complaints. Our worlds do not rotate on their bowel habits, sexual dysfunction, or relationship issues. It's vexing that not answering strangers' questions often leads to increased persistence in seeking answers: the newly introduced golfer I don't know and will never see again will inevitably try harder to get their questions addressed! Why do some feel entitled to a discussion? We always try our best to help...but when appropriate and for those we share a friendship. Just as I won't ask for legal, accounting, or investment advice from someone I don't know, be respectful of our playing time. If we choose to be part of a discussion about your health, you will know. But if we don't engage, let it go.

# Part II
# Mechanics and Performance

# Chapter 5
## *What's Going On (in the swing)*

As with most things we do in life, there is usually a means of maximum efficiency to achieve almost any goal. Unfortunately, there are many more ways to fail. And, as we have all experienced, learning how to identify the means or method that works best for each of us can often be immensely difficult. It may ultimately be deemed impossible for some. As one observes an expert downhill skier glide down a mountain, the skier appears to be expending so little excessive energy–they are using minimal movement while achieving maximal speed. But there is more going on than just speed. The expert skier also demonstrates a noticeable elegance in their motion–no extraneous movement. On the other hand, as we observe a novice skiing down a 'bunny hill' with a small angle of incline, he or she seems to flail–first turning excessively to the right and then using way too much compensatory effort to turn back to the left. The beginning skier doesn't quite know how much effort to expend at which precise moment as they make exaggerated movements to control their speed and trajectory. There is so much wasted movement as the new skier is using his or her arms, legs, and body in contorted maneuvers to maintain balance. The novice skier struggles with rhythm and cadence, unsure whether to trust or fear gravity, while the expert glides effortlessly without concern.

This concept applies similarly to the hand movements of skilled surgeons. One of the most basic skills a surgeon must learn in training is how to tie a surgical knot. Unlike tying a regular knot, say on your shoe, a surgical knot must be absolutely precise. It must be tied in a manner that will not loosen or become undone—nor can it be too tight that it causes damage to the tissue it is holding together. The knot must often be tied in a very small space—sometimes with the surgeon unable to observe the suture material or even his hands as he is tying the critical knot. The knot must be tied quickly and without undue wasted time or movement. The novice surgical intern ties surgical knots with large hand, arm, and even shoulder and body movements, as he or she tries to control the thin, slippery, suture material. Through multiple latex gloves, they do their best to tie a knot in the mandated seconds—often unsuccessfully. Tying a surgical knot—under pressure, is a challenging skill to learn. Observing an expert surgeon in an operating room can be described as a ballet of hand movement—refined, smooth, and efficient. The seasoned surgeon has almost no arm motion at all. The suture is manipulated purely within his or her fingers as the surgeon's arms and body never seem to move up or down. This principle applies to skilled musicians and artists as well—efficiency of motion with minimal nonproductive activity.

The golf swing is no different. Go to any driving range and observe the line-up of golfers trying to improve their games. Without even watching where the ball flies–or doesn't, you can sit down and observe just the swing. Without understanding proper golf mechanics, you can see quiet fluidity, efficiency, and minimal effort utilized by the advanced golfer. Better yet, close your eyes and listen to the sound of the ball being struck. As the expert player swings, the acceleration of the club makes a swoosh sound in the air. As the club strikes the golf ball, there is a sharp snap, and the descending blow of the club causes a rapid compression of the ball. Now, if you really concentrate, you could probably hear the ball spin in the air as it takes off the clubface. The properly struck ball simply makes a different sound than one that is hit clunkily. The swing of a talented golfer is efficient–the legs, arms, and core work as a coordinated unit–perfect in their synchronization. The beginning player will do whatever he or she can to move the club harder and faster– but the flight of the ball will often be inconsistent and unpredictable. Direction and distance are entities for the new golfer that rarely go as intended.

Novice players are often identifiable by their tendency to move their entire body without proper sequencing, attempting to hit the ball rather than allowing the club to swing. In the incorrect thought processes of the beginner, the means to get the ball up in the air must, of course, be done with maximal effort. In the beginner's mind, harder means farther. Nothing could be further from the actual reality of how to properly hit a golf ball. They don't comprehend that stroke consistency and, ultimately, desired ball flight will be produced by a more smoothly synchronized movement than one that is predicated purely on power and effort. Watching professional golfers, we notice their powerful swings, prompting us to try to replicate their motion. They may be exerting a significant amount of effort–but only because they have mastered the synchronization learned from the proper technique from years earlier. More power will ultimately be generated from proper swing mechanics than could ever be generated from muscular strength.

### *But what is really going on?*

Obviously, we are not golf pros. However, we are observers and will try to explain some of the key mechanical events that occur during a golf swing. Not every coach has to have been a player. Often, people can understand things they may not be able to perform. Having a brief description of swing mechanics will help as we continue to analyze the golfer and the game. Believe it or not, what occurs in the golf swing has applications to other aspects of our lives. Bear with us, and you will see.

To understand the physics of a golf swing, we must consider the mechanics of rotational motion. Consider, for example, a ball at the end of an attached string: When an object travels around in a circle, it moves outward. Within the principles of physics, this event has been labeled *centrifugal force*. Centrifugal force is the outward force away from the axis of rotation acting on a revolving object. If we apply this principle to the golf swing, we note the following: As a player performs his or her backswing, the club is essentially rotated around the player. With the arms extended and the wrists cocked, the player's weight is transferred onto his trail side. As the golfer transitions into his forward movement–initiated by the lower body and core, the player's arms will follow. If the arms are kept in the rotational axis as the body turns forward, the player will replicate a consistent release point at the bottom of the swing–the club now acting as an extension of the extended player's arms. Assuming posture and body position have been maintained, contact with the ball is made. The true key is the line of action of the impact force that must pass through the center of mass of the club head (something we also refer to as the sweet spot). During impact, the force exerted on the club head by the shaft is negligible compared to the impact force between the club head and the ball. Thus, during impact, the club head can be thought of as a free body (such as the ball on the string, as previously described). What is most important to understand is that the arms and wrists play a somewhat passive role in the swing *force*. Obviously, these structures play a role in 'control' of the swing (but do not play an active role in the swing itself). The actual swing energy comes from the movement of the torso and shoulders, which, when properly sequenced from the swing initiation from the core and lower body, quickly accentuate and rotate the golfer's arm and club through the swing. This biomechanical event has been studied extensively:[2]

# What's Going On (in the swing)

## Impulse of a force

Let's now examine the collision between the club and the golf ball. Given a force that varies over time, which acts on a body for a finite time interval:

$$\Delta t = t_f - t_i$$

Force impulse is the physical vector quantity I:

$$\bar{I} = \int_{t_i}^{t_f} \bar{F}(t)dt$$

The unit of measurement of the pulse is kg (m / s2) s = kg (m / s). Applying Newton's II law we obtain:

$$\bar{I} = \int_{t_i}^{t_f} \bar{F}(t)dt = \int_{t_i}^{t_f} \frac{d\bar{q}}{dt}dt =$$

$$= \int_{t_i}^{t_f} d\bar{q} = \bar{q}_2 - \bar{q}_1 = \Delta\bar{q}$$

Therefore, the impulse of the resultant of the forces acting on a body in a time interval $\Delta t$ is equal to the variation of the momentum of the body in the interval $\Delta t$. In a collision, the two interacting bodies exert forces on each other that vary rapidly over time (impulsive forces). It is quite simple to calculate, for example, the modulus of the average force acting on the ball in the interval $\Delta t$ s, relative to the impact between a club and a golf ball. We have the following starting data:

- mass of the ball (m) = 50 g (weight force P = 0.5N);
- initial speed Vi = 40 m / s;
- duration of contact between the club and the ball $\Delta t$ = 1 ms.

A launch of this type could have a range of about 150 m. The initial momentum of the ball is 0.

$$F \, \Delta t = \Delta q = mV_i \text{ -0}$$

$$F = (mV_i) / \Delta t \approx 2000 \text{ N}$$

and finally:

$$F/mg \approx 4000$$

In the interval $\Delta t$ the impulsive force acting on the ball is extremely high and the other external forces present are negligible. Precisely for this reason, this is an impulsive approximation. The golf ball feels stiff. But, during the impact with the club, it can deform by up to 2 cm. The ball is made of elastic material and follows, with good approximation, Hooke's law with an elastic constant of 760000 N / m.

- "r" is the radius of the golfer's swing;
- "P" is the position of the handle on which the golfer takes the club;
- "G" is the center of gravity of the golf club;
- "LG" is the distance from "P" to the center of mass "G" of the golf club;
- "θ" is the swing angle that the golfer's arms form with the vertical;
- "α" is the angle the golf club makes with the golfer's arms.

The position of the center of mass can be expressed with the following relations:

$$x = -r\sin\theta + l_G \sin(\theta + \alpha)$$
$$y = r\cos\theta - l_G \cos(\theta + \alpha)$$

And using Newton's second law we can write the general equation of force in the x direction:

$$\sum F_x = m \cdot a_{Gx}$$

where:

- "sum Fx" is the sum of the forces in the x direction;
- "m" is the mass of the stick;
- "aGx" is the acceleration of the center of mass in the x direction, with respect to the ground.

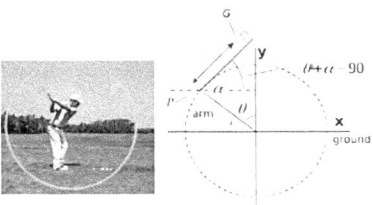

---

2  From: Physics in Golf, Giovanni Di Maria, 2021, EEWeb

So, what does all this mean?

First, removing the advanced mathematics, it means anything that interrupts the natural sequencing of the centrifugal force already in action as the club is moving toward the ball will be destructive. Your intentions to 'help it' with additional effort will most likely interrupt the flow of energy already accelerating the club head as it is in a collision path with the ball. So don't get in the way! Doing so will only bring havoc to a natural system that is doing just fine on its own.

Interestingly, I had the opportunity to observe my 7-year-old great-nephew swing a golf club. His parents wanted him to start learning the game, and I observed him handling the club when it was placed into his little hand. I noted something quite interesting: Like all children his age, he had limited upper-body strength. Indeed, when he was handed the club, he had difficulty lifting it above his head–the clubhead was heavy relative to his size and strength. As he was instructed to try to swing the club back, it was apparent to me he did so with his *lower body!* He didn't have the arm or shoulder strength to actually swing the club back, but he could rotate his pelvis to do so. His stronger *lower body* was doing the work! With enough rotation, the club went back. Being attached (held) by his hands and then through his arms, the club then went up. The club had nowhere else to go but to follow the path defined by his body movement and physical configuration! Without any instruction, he innately used his lower body to 'swing' the club. By doing so, he could more easily swing the relatively heavy club without interference or influence from his hands or arms. As he gradually gained more experience (practice) with this lower body rotation, the club movement became more fluid. He was able to strike the ball quite well without upper-body interference. Perhaps as we learn how to move and navigate within the world, starting as toddlers, we observe that accomplishing a task involving *force* generally requires us to push or pull harder. This is generally effective in moving something in front of us. But to move an object *around* us, the natural forces of movement in a circle–*centrifugal force,* is different. The actual amount of force or effort is important, but it will be wasted if the direction of movement is altered. Stay out of the way to let it happen.

This crucial concept, central to the power of a golf swing, isn't typically learned or applied well by adults new to the game. As adults, we try to use our upper body to move an object regardless of direction–straight or circular. Adults new to the game will (mistakenly) apply learned experiences from other endeavors; to hit a golf ball far, the new player thinks he or she needs to try to help it along with the upper body. In the golf swing, this application of power only results in more effort being expended with damaging results. Perhaps this is why golfers who learned the game when young generally become better players.

Perhaps one of the most elusive aspects of learning the golf swing is that it is also counterintuitive. This means that, in many ways, understanding how to properly hit the golf ball defies what we consider *obvious*. For instance, in normal activities, such as hitting a baseball into the air, one would wind up the bat and strike the ball from low to high. Trying to strike from underneath would be an obvious method to elevate the baseball. If a player wanted to hit a tennis ball high in the air for a lob, they would keep the racquet below the ball and strike the ball while raising the racquet from low to high.

But to hit a golf ball high into the air requires something else–the player needs to strike the ball in a manner that maximizes the loft you present to the ball at impact. Remember our description of the golf club loft in Chapter 1? We were discussing how a player can choose how much loft or angle the face of the club has. This will impact the launch angle of the ball once a club impacts it. A more open face (more loft) can propel a ball higher in the air than a less lofted club. Hitting a ball properly to maximize the dynamic loft of the club requires making square contact with the ball before the club hits the ground. Importantly, one does not want to scoop or try to lift the ball up with the club. The club will make contact with the ball as it moves forward and slightly down. You could walk onto any driving range and identify the beginning players as they make a great effort to *lift* the ball into the air rather than swing through it. Some of the more intuitive players will eventually realize their efforts to lift the ball by swinging up are ineffective. Others will never gain this perspective. Instead, they try not only to lift the ball but also, with increased frustration, to hit the golf ball harder. Needless to say, this is not a good combination of energy exertion. Lifting and hitting harder will, however, provide excellent exercise and possibly fulfill both aerobic and anaerobic movement requirements for the day.

Another misconception regarding the proper contact of the club and ball is also seen quite frequently on a driving range filled with beginners: to hit the ball farther, they try to swing faster. Visit any municipal range where many of the participants have not had professional lessons or qualified instruction. Look for the gaggle of young men, all of whom could easily play for a high school or college football team. Without proper instruction, their attempt to hit the ball farther—perhaps into the stratosphere, is to swing the club as hard and fast as they possibly can. Just observing their efforts causes one to have a twinge of pain in the lower back region. Having witnessed this misconception many times, sometimes I thought I might pop a vertebral disc just through observation. But despite their failures, they keep trying harder and harder to do the same thing. The physics of the proper golf swing simply doesn't work that way: Power swinging a golf club does not necessarily translate into the distance or height the ball will travel. Conversely, power generated incorrectly leads to more frustration than pleasure.

The game is challenging enough with its rules, expected etiquette, and mandatory clothing requirements. Learning how to simply not get in the way should be easy enough! But it obviously isn't. Staying down through the ball as simple physics takes over shouldn't be all that hard–yet it appears to be so for so many of us. Perhaps this is best described as knowing when to *hold on and when to let go*. We need to *hold on* to properly align the club in the right swing path as we begin the backswing and then subsequently load the coiled body to be ready for release. But, when the club swings forward, the player must *let go*. He or she must allow the kinetic energy (the energy an object has because of its motion) created by the club head's position and the body rotation moving that club head–to continue without interference or additional 'influence.' Relying on our muscles to accelerate the club is actually weaker and less reproducible than the natural centrifugal forces that result from a properly sequenced swing. Trying to use upper body strength to increase club speed actually interferes and slows down the swing. Similarly, our ability to time 'muscle assistance' in the swing is less consistent than letting the natural swing forces follow their path. *Holding on and letting go.* It's not an easy physical or mental thing to do. But isn't this true about our world outside of golf as well? We will explore this concept outside the links shortly.

# Chapter 6

## *Training Aids: Help Or Hindrance?*

Once, I encountered a golfer—actually, quite skilled—who declared he'd spare no expense to enhance his golfing prowess. I met him years ago when I was just starting to play the game, and I remember laughing at his suggestion. I can easily recall how I listened (half-heartedly) as he described the costly, time-consuming efforts he had gone through to shave a few strokes off his score and improve his distance and accuracy. He spent tens of thousands of dollars on golf lessons with a variety of instructors–each offering the magic cure to his swing woes. In addition to the lesson expenditures, the addicted golfer purchased new clubs whenever his favorite equipment brand introduced a new line (which was practically every season). And, of course, he had a closet, garage, and basement full of the latest gadgetry and training aids designed to turn him into the golfer he aspired to be–or so they advertised.

As we played our round together, my new friend described all the efforts he had put forth in his quest to achieve his golf skills. He was a talented player, yet all his 'extreme' efforts appeared quite over the top to me. I mean, he was really a good player...where did he expect to go with his game? Eventually, I understood his attempts to master the game to be reflective of a rather sinister situation: he was absolutely obsessed with buying or doing whatever was necessary to make him a better golfer. However, the real question that needed to be addressed was how he, and in the broader sense, how we golfers define what makes us *better*. Better is an elusive term that may have similarities to a bottomless pit.

As I observed and listened to his description of his obsession with the game, I started wondering more about what I was witnessing. Was he looking for the skills and tools to allow him to strike the ball better? To lower his scores? Or, and perhaps most importantly, was he looking for a means to enjoy the game more? I was struggling to understand, in the context of golf, what defined *better*. After completing one of our rounds, I realized he was only interested in one thing: lowering his scores to *beat* his fellow players. He wasn't striving to play better for self-improvement's sake, or to relish the learning process and mastering a challenging skill. Nope. For this player, the joy of the game was secondary to accomplishing *that* specific objective: to beat his friends and those he played with. It wasn't monetarily driven–it was purely a need to satisfy his ego and to feel he was on top. In my limited analysis of this person, I didn't initially recognize his uncontrollable competitiveness. He simply needed to win.

I came to the realization this individual would never fully understand or enjoy the game. No matter how much time or money he spent on endless lessons or new equipment, he would be in a constant quest for the impossible: there is never a low enough score. I can't think of a single golfer I ever met who felt he or she was playing at the level that met their expectations. For some, there is always more, and never enough. Which, for the sake of self-improvement, I guess is a good thing. But expending so much time, effort, and money to fulfill the primary goal of being on top of the little hill of your golf club membership without experiencing a sense of accomplishment is truly quite sad. For some, there will never be a moment of joy (in the game) except when winning. And most of us don't or can't win all the time. This perspective leaves our player in a constant struggle to achieve, interrupted by only episodic moments of feeling joy and success. This appears to be a frustrating means to an end.

Capitalizing on the needs of the compulsive golfer, there are an apparently infinite number of training aids and devices designed to *help* the golfer reach his or her potential. So, what were these training aids my avid playing partner invested so much time and hard-earned money in? Ever aware there are players who will never reach a plateau of satisfaction, there is no shortage of devices and swing aids to the rescue. An Amazon Fulfillment Center probably does not have enough shelf space to house all the gizmos and gadgets that are available. Fortunately, for the support of the economy, players keep buying this stuff!

**Putting Aids:** Their need is obvious as we try in vain to master the proper technique to strike the motionless 1.68" ball into the mouth of the 4.25" wide golf hole. Just watch enough golf on television, and you'll see a wealth of these devices for sale. Somehow, the propensity of the advertisements for these miracle devices seems to be during the late-night hours. Maybe at that time of day, we are more vulnerable and likely to take the plunge and buy one. However, the concept of purchasing a putting aid this way seems like folly from the get-go. Similarly, trying to buy such devices online or in a store *without proper guidance or instruction* appears unlikely to work.

The reason for their failure appears rather basic: After years of integrating visual, haptic, proprioceptive, and balance experiences into one's neural network, each of us experiences the world slightly differently. We share the same sense receptors and integrative neuroanatomy, but some of us are more visually oriented, and others are more kinesthetically sensitive. Some golfers need to hear the sound of the ball as it strikes the putter (or club face), while others need to feel it. Some golfers see the undulations on the green as a series of straight lines, and others see the subtleties as a compilation of curves. Some golfers putt looking down at the ball, while others look at the hole or with their eyes closed. Some golfers stand upright, others are bent. (The LPGA star Michelle Wie West putted with her waist bent nearly 90 degrees). Some golfers putt with their left hand low, others with their hands right-hand low. Given such variation of player perceptions and capabilities and given the myriad of putting techniques that can be utilized, it seems impossible that *a* putting training device will be applicable to all of us–or any of us. Simply buying a putting training aid without an understanding of how one *perceives* the putting surface will lead to a failure of expectation. And the failure may not be the golfer can't putt properly. Rather, it may be as simple as the training aid isn't right for his or her perceptual needs or deficiencies.

For example, I was once shown how to shoot a rifle. The person instructing me was adept at this skill and was insistent that I follow his instructions to the letter. I did everything the instructor told me, yet nearly every shot I made was off the mark. I became increasingly frustrated, as did the instructor. Was the problem my eyesight? Not at all, it was 20/20. I held the rifle steady and aimed at the target–but I always missed. The instructor eventually walked away, thinking he had the worst student he had ever seen. And then I tried something else–I moved the rifle to my other shoulder. With the instructor trying all types of maneuvers to get me to aim the rifle properly, the one thing he didn't account for was how my brain actually perceived the world through the scope of the gun. I'm right-handed–but my dominant eye is my *left*. Once I moved the rifle to my left side (and didn't copy exactly what the instructor did), I struck the target quite consistently. With the rifle on my left shoulder, I was using my dominant left eye to aim. As good as the instructor's technique was, he ignored a critical yet simple component of how my visual cortex integrated with the world. There was nothing wrong with the rifle, me, or my vision. It was simply a matter of knowing how I 'work.'  In retrospect, it was disappointing that he never considered this as a possible cause for my missed shots. An instructor is only as good as their experience. A training device applied without regard to whom it *should* be used can have the same bad consequences–or worse.

Similarly, the concept of selling putting-training devices to the masses of players on television or the Internet–with the number of individual variables of perception and skills involved, seems doomed from the get-go. Just walk onto a practice putting green at any club–public or private, and you'll find an array of tools and aids to assist golfers in sinking putts. As I observe serious, focused, golfers placing mirrors, countless tees, rulers, and other oddly shaped gizmos and objects on the practice putting surface, I am amazed. There's a guy in the corner of the practice green with a laser attached to his putter. There appears to be no end to the development, marketing, and sale of putting training aids. But, how to prove or disprove the latest innovation in putting training has an actual benefit is challenging to prove or disprove. Assuming only good intentions, a new device may work for the person who invented it, but for it to work for others, they, too, must see and feel the putting surface the same way. Perhaps the failing golfer is 'left-eyed' as well, and the training device he or she is working with will never accommodate that. We each experience and take in the world differently. How can someone else's training aid design be applicable to all of us? It simply can't. Before depending on one of the many putting aids available, first discuss it with someone who understands your individual tendencies and needs. Most importantly, understand there isn't a quick solution to a complicated skill such as putting.

While on the topic of putting aids...

Looking at the actual putters that are available today creates an additional level of confusion. Just as we all have individual putting idiosyncrasies, putter designs vary more than any other club in our bag. Walk into any large golf superstore and observe the putting area stocked with an array of the latest putters available–it's a dizzying display of chrome shafts, odd shapes, and enticing colors. The shaft length, club weight, and head design all come in countless styles. You could try a new putter every day, but you still have hundreds to choose from. And despite the physical differences, they all will roll the ball. The differences between each putter may be quite subtle as you try one after another. Finding the right putter takes time, practice, and patience. Mesmerized by the new-fangled putting devices whose heads are composed of multiple inlays and materials, you decide to pick up the most appealing putter to try out. And a funny thing happens–somehow, in the store, the golf balls seem to effortlessly find their way into the plastic hole on the plastic mat. That is until you take the newly purchased $500 toy out to the course. Now, suddenly, the putter's magic is gone.

Funny, how with all the putting-training devices available and all the types of putters one can buy–and seeing so many players practice with them, why do I constantly see so many shitty putts by those dedicated players? It simply can't be because the training aids don't work. It's also highly unlikely there's a deficiency in the putter you selected at the store. Don't become *that guy* with 30 putters in his closet and just as many putting training aids. Obviously, it isn't the putter, and it isn't the new toy on the practice range that will make you better. The key to good putting is to learn to work with how *you* see and feel the world–not using someone else's perception of how you should. Understand that no training aid or putter will work for you if it isn't designed to accommodate your needs or tendencies. It doesn't matter how much it costs or who endorses it. The training aid and putter must be right for you. Given the importance of the putter, be patient with yourself in finding the right one. If you are truly serious about getting better, have yourself evaluated on a putting analyzer or see a golf professional who can objectively assess what you are doing while putting. Then, pick a putter that feels right in your hands, looks good to your eye, and practice with it. Importantly, don't fall for the latest ingenious putting aid advertised at midnight.

**Ball striking aids:** After nearly 30 years of playing the game, I've had many golf lessons in my life. By no means am I a lesson-hound: I don't take a lesson every week. Maybe six or so lessons a year seems to be the right number for me–a few in the off-season, at the start, and a couple during mid-season. It takes me weeks to months to integrate the lesson into my subconscious. Taking more lessons than that, and I'm just wasting money. However, there are those golfers who take lessons more regularly and find a benefit to them. Whatever it takes each player to accomplish their objective is probably the best advice. I have also learned that we each see and hear things from various instructors differently. Perhaps they are all saying the same thing to you...but you respond or integrate the instructions better from some rather than others. If you're taking those frequent lessons and you aren't achieving the skills or playing the quality of game you are *realistically* seeking, perhaps changing the routine–or instructor might be helpful.

One of the things that has always struck me as odd in trying to improve is the number and variety of ball-striking aids available. Like the putting aids, television and the Internet are ripe with an array of golf gizmos. I have no issue with the attempt to design devices to improve a golfer's swing. But knowing which device is best for which swing problem is something most golfers simply don't know. It's awfully difficult to be objective about one's swing–and what needs correction. The best intended or designed device used by someone with a swing issue unrelated to the capabilities of the device is just wasted effort. Unless someone who is knowledgeably skilled is observing you, it's very difficult to properly understand what's occurring in your swing. Indeed, it's challenging to know what's inhibiting your game. One size rarely fits all, and a training aid simply can't be purchased based on a slick advertisement (complete with testimonials) with the expectation that it will autocorrect what's wrong with a player's swing.

Many of us have likely seen the golf film *Tin Cup*, where Rene Russo takes a driving range lesson with Kevin Costner. Costner's character, laden with swing aids on each limb and his head, tries to work through his swing issues. Do they help? Like everything else, the device is only useful if used properly and consistently for the *exact problem* they were designed for. Somehow, I see golfers bring out the latest gadget one day, only to be replaced the next with something else. I'm sure there is science and validation to show how some of these devices work. I'm also sure there is a multi-million-dollar advertising and sales industry involved in the marketing and distribution of these devices. I think finding a qualified instructor who can observe your swing and can *communicate* what he or she identifies as your problem is a much more worthwhile means to improve your game. And, like everything else, there are all types of instructors...one doesn't need to be a PGA pro to give advice. The guy who delivers my morning paper will give me swing recommendations–all I need to do is ask him.

There was a golf 'pro' at a driving range I used frequently to practice. Fortunately, he is no longer around. Every time I would walk past his teaching *spot*, I would see another gadget: a bigger Hula-hoop, an object that resembled an oversized tennis racquet, a myriad of colored sticks, flexible bands, and objects to be placed near the player's feet, legs, waist, shoulders, or head. There were things to be strapped on, things to be laced up, things to be attached, and things that, well, I'm honestly not quite sure where some of them were to be placed or used. Once, I observed a lesson from a distance, and I wasn't sure if the student was learning how to swing a golf club or become a participant in a circus. I remember looking at the disheartened student as she had more junk on and around her that I don't even think she *could* swing the club! The instructor was more engaged with the *stuff* and what it was supposed to do than he was with what the student was accomplishing. Not once did he look at *her* and see the look of absolute frustration on the student's face. The instructor was focused on the swing training aids and what they were telling him, but not on her. He was distracted from observing what the player was doing. Was the problem the training aids? No. It was the fault of who was directing their use. An aid for anything is only as good as the *appropriate* application of its use. Perhaps this is anecdotal, but when I learned how to ride a bike, I got on the bike. I also fell off quite a few times before I mastered it. To learn to ski downhill, I had to get on my skis. I taught surgery to hundreds of students and residents. I did so by giving them the instruments and carefully observing them. Obviously, they were only allowed to do limited things. So why, with golf, are there so many *aids?* Why are there so many devices that are an adjunct to the swing? From my perspective, any device placed as an intermediary between the student and the club only seems to separate what they need to experience in the golf swing. A question should be asked regarding the use of swing aids: Are the teaching aids forcing the student-player to *think* too much about the device as opposed to facilitating the student to *feel* and *focus* on the actual swing? Are the devices causing too much *overthinking* and not enough *feeling* during the swing? Somehow, an intermediary aid seems to interfere with that process. But despite all the aids available–and there are many, I really think the key to improvement is finding a golf instructor who understands your swing–and your limits. Don't stop looking for him or her until you find them. And when you do, don't let go.

The bottom line: We all love the gadgets, the gizmos, and the equipment in this game. As technology and innovation advance, we want to participate in the evolution and use modern tools that will help us achieve our goals. But often, we get lost looking for a solution without precisely understanding the problem. Knowing which tool you need is really a difficult question that must be addressed. Unless you just enjoy buying and having more stuff, it probably makes more practical sense to spend the money on lessons from someone you trust and then practice what you were taught. If the (qualified) instructor feels a particular training aid would be beneficial, then go for it. Finding a good instructor can be challenging, but a great teacher can see and do so much to help you improve and enjoy the game. Remember, there is no easy fix to this game...unless you consider a lobotomy an option.

# Chapter 7
## *Get Real, And Don't Force It*

With golf, I can't think of any other physical activity I have worked so long and so hard to master, but I constantly feel I am still learning the basics. And despite being a reasonably good golfer (at least through the prism of my peers), each time I step onto the practice range, I must mentally rehearse my swing to strike the ball properly. I wish this sequencing was ingrained into my neuro-muscular 'memory,' but it isn't. I must work at it each and every time. Maybe that's because I learned the game as an adult and not as a child, and my swing did not have the necessary time and rehearsals to solidify the proper sequencing. Perhaps it's because the golf swing is an unnatural movement for me, and it will unlikely ever be something I can perform without significant focus and concentration. Whatever the myriad reasons, I must repeatedly tender and tinker with my swing to get it right. There's a constant battle between what my head and body are trying to do. The game requires so much effort for me to be reasonably proficient that I've accepted that the proper golf swing just doesn't come easily for me.

Despite the significant effort, time, and cost required, and as much as one can rehearse and practice, review, study, and then rinse and repeat this learning process, a committed golfer will consistently feel he or she has the ability to perform as desired. Golfers are a tough lot, and they don't give up on their efforts easily. After all, I *once* hit that 7-iron 185 yards. So why, when I'm out on the golf course, shouldn't I use positive thinking and believe I can repeat that same shot? Why do I repeatedly forget (or ignore?) all my mis-hits on the range or recall that my average 7-iron distance is not 185 yards but more like 160 yards? Why, when approaching the green after a good drive, do I next grab the club that can produce the distance I *could* hit but often don't? Similarly, why do most golfers play from tee boxes that are much too long for their true abilities? Why do we golf with the feeling we can play at a higher level that, realistically, is more of an exception rather than the rule? These are questions we should all ask ourselves as we honestly assess our games.

As obsessed golfers, most of us are guilty of overestimating our potential while simultaneously possessing a misunderstanding of our true abilities. On the tee box, my regular drive length is about 240 yards, yet perhaps one out of ten times, I can hit the drive 260 yards. So why did I go for 'it' trying to hit over the water in front of me rather than take a bail-out? I can barely hit the ball over the water in front of me, yet each time I try, it's as though I have amnesia from all my previous failed attempts. Because of my failure to consider my real skill level, I end up plunking the ball into the water (again), and I shoot a double bogey for the effort. Why did I not pay attention to my drives on the range and know the odds of success were against me? If I were at a blackjack or craps table, I would never take a long-shot bet–unless the outcome didn't matter. However, on the golf course, the miscalculation of ability *always* has an outcome that matters. Why do we constantly overestimate our skill level? Let's look at a more extreme example of this.

I have a very good friend who also happens to be a very bad golfer. Bad is an understatement of his inability to play the game; he's absolutely terrible. If I played as poorly as he does, I would most likely quit the game, sell my clubs, and take up cliff diving. The experience of striking a large rock at the bottom of the cliff would be less painful than continuing to play golf at his level. I suspect if he kept an accurate handicap index, it would be somewhere around the highest allowable–which happens to be 54. Playing with him is simply a nightmare to observe...but he is my friend, and I do enjoy his company. On a *good* day, he might lose two dozen balls while playing a round–I'm not kidding. And yet, almost in a Charlie Brown way, he always comes prepared for the onslaught with a good attitude. I have never seen him run out of golf balls despite his inability to hit the ball somewhere within the zip code of the fairway. I think his golf bag was specially made to be bottomless–he just keeps pulling out more balls to whack away at as his shots fly wayward, never to be seen again. It is truly a painful sight to watch.

Not only does he not know how to use a club properly, but he has an internal debate with himself over each shot–it takes him a while to pick out the *perfect* club. In the end, it really doesn't matter–the shot will be pathetically bad. I play with him because he is my friend, and I suspect nobody else would tolerate his lack of skill or his failure to understand he has no skill. I have suggested lessons, but he never has the time. I have suggested he practice, but his schedule is too overloaded. Every time he asks to play, I know I'm in for a painful day. Perhaps out of pity or guilt, I agree. And so, on a beautiful summer day, we played.

By about the third hole, the collection of golfers behind us began to hurl insults at our lack of forward progress. Undeterred by their expletives, my friend announced to me he was going to "draw his next shot over the tree or fade it over the water." In other words, he will try to 'work' or manipulate the ball to fly a particular way in the air. This is a difficult task for even an accomplished golfer. *Seriously, that's what you are about to try?* I asked myself.

80

"How about simply trying to make contact with the ball, get it off the ground and into the air for starters?" I replied. After his usual protracted amount of time, my friend hit a worm-burner inches above the ground. The streaking ball struck a tree root that redirected the ball into a parked golf cart. The uncontrolled flying object then careened into a nearby pond as the occupants of the golf cart glared back at us. I'm not quite sure if their gaze was one of fear or anger–perhaps it was a bit of both with a touch of dismay. With my buddy's lack of ability to track the ball as it ricocheted back and forth (his vision is not the best), he announced proudly what a fine shot it was! I questioned many times if he was truly blind or just completely out of touch with what occurred around him. Perhaps visual impairment is a small part of the problem, but his failure to appreciate his lack of skill is most likely the main culprit. The rest of the round was a basic rinse-and-repeat of this episode.

Obviously, my miscalculation of a club's shot distance is a far more subtle overestimation of skill than someone who is clueless on the course. The relevancy of describing my friend's lack of playing ability is that it is another, if not slightly exaggerated, example of a golfer being unrealistic about his or her goals and skills.

My suspicion is that if my golf buddy wouldn't confuse golf *capabilities* with his known *abilities,* trying to 'bend' the ball

81

around obstacles wouldn't even be in his spectrum of consideration. Honestly, he frequently informs me of his intent on every tee box to score a birdie. If he would focus on the basics without even thinking about the score on every hole (he's lucky to make a triple bogey on most occasions), he'd be a much more satisfied golfer. But for him, the score is important. He fails to understand a better score will follow good swing basics and technique rather than trying a hero shot each and every time.

Working with what you have at each level of the game should be key. If my friend tried to play *within* himself, he might recognize there is potential for real improvement, and taking lessons and actually practicing would be the proper way to go about this game. How many golfers spend ridiculous efforts trying to 'bend it' rather than taking what skill level they have and working with it? On a larger scale, outside of golf, how often do we spend our efforts trying to resolve a problem by forcing a solution without a foundational understanding of the question? We should be spending most of our time and effort trying to grasp what the problem is–the solution will often present itself.

As I observe golfers on a driving range–men, women, old and young, I generally see one thing in common: They all want to hit the ball far. Okay, I get that. And, as Homo sapiens has evolved as a species, we have innately learned that to hit something farther, we must generally put more energy into it. I see the golfers on the range swing as hard as they can. The big, brawny fellow who looks as though he could throw a railroad tie across the road holds the golf club like it's a toothpick in his bear-sized hand. Using all his 350 lbs., he swings with the power and might of a lumberjack, and...he pounds the ball...into the ground. Despite his huge windup and release of the club, the poorly struck ball dribbles harmlessly about 30 yards into the grass in front of him. Realizing the ball didn't go very far, he immediately thinks swinging harder is better. Rather than reconsider the effort and outcome he just expended, the huge fella thinks it's better to try harder with his next swing–and so on. He keeps beating the ball, and on occasion, it looks as though it will hit the sun. His occasional success reinforces his activity. Next to the huge fella, a teenager is practicing. He can whip his lithe frame around in a manner that would cause something in my body to herniate. The lad strikes the ball with such speed it hurts just to observe him. His ball is hit uncontrollably into the stratosphere–sometimes it goes right, and sometimes it goes left. But the middle of the driving range–where he is apparently aiming, is foreign to him. None of these want-to-be golfers takes the time to assess what they are doing wrong. Harder and faster must be the answer to getting the ball farther and higher...right?

But if you look closely at the array of golfers at the range, someone does stick out. It's the young lady who looks as though she weighs about 90 lbs. She isn't swinging hard, and she isn't swinging fast. She isn't *forcing* anything. She is quietly swinging the club within her ability to control the club *without making any effort to control it.* This is a seemingly contradictory process: control by not controlling. She is letting the natural energy of rotational movement–by proper timing and sequencing of her motions, to *allow the club* to provide the energy to get the ball up into the air. We discussed this phenomenon in Chapter 5, and here it is playing out. This young golfer has learned that without being particularly fast or strong, and despite her small stature, she can efficiently swing the club–*without force.* The physics of her impact is effective in achieving her goal. She not only hits the ball a very reasonable distance, but she does so consistently and repeatedly.

The takeaway from this discussion is obvious: take what you have, and don't force it. A good golf swing looks effortless. But the more important thing is that it *feels* effortless. That's because, as the 90 lb. young woman has learned (or more likely simply experienced), the most efficient creation of power has to do with storing up energy in the backswing and then sequentially surrendering to gravitational forces and momentum in the transition to the downswing. She needs to get the club back and, essentially, let it go through impact as the club will follow the path set for it. This can't be forced, nor can it be rushed. There is tension and release; *holding on and letting go:* Allow the natural feedback loop of sequential movement to be the guide. Remember, we're not all equally gifted, but with dedication and hard work, most of us can improve. If you can minimize the pressure to get quick results and focus on the granular process, real progress can emerge. But more challenging for us all is to realistically assess abilities–both mentally and physically. Apply yourself in a manner that is properly sequenced and efficient. Use those assessments not just to play golf but to succeed in all aspects of your life. Perhaps you will find it takes less effort than you anticipated, with a far better outcome. Efficiency over power will often be the most effective means to achieve many of our goals.

# Chapter 8
## *Play Within Yourself*

One of the hardest lessons we all must learn at some point or another is to play within ourselves. Perhaps that lesson is easier to discuss or write about than it is to accept and achieve. We all aspire to do well and reach our goals–especially at work and, ideally, at play. We observe our environment and others within it, and then plan to succeed in what we value or have an obligation to achieve. One of the most challenging aspects of achievement, however, is understanding our limitations.

I watch golf on television–a lot. It's not that I don't have anything else to do, but like so many others, I learn by repetition, and professional golfers are the epitome of that. Watch a video replay of any golfer at the pro level, and each swing appears nearly identical. And side-by-side analysis video replays of nearly any professional golfer will reveal only the most subtle of changes. They are absolute robots with a golf club. I have often observed the new young players on the circuit; six-foot-three, thin-as-a-rail studs, effortlessly smack the golf ball well over 330 yards while splitting the fairway in half. For the non-golfing readers, this would be a feat the rest of us can only dream about. After watching extraordinarily high levels of golf swing execution on television, I am often motivated to take additional golf lessons.

One of my worst golf learning experiences (with whom I later learned to be an inexperienced instructor) occurred when the instructor observed my swing and then pulled out a paper fold-out sequence of Dustin Johnson's positions throughout his swing. For the uninitiated, Johnson is a very accomplished professional golfer. Why this golf teacher chose to use the sequencing of Johnson's swing as an instructional aid *for me* is beyond my comprehension. This is not a discussion on whether one should like or dislike Dustin Johnson, but in the world of golf, Johnson's golf swing is the envy of many. He is a talented player who can hit the ball into tomorrow. In this lifetime, with my current (and most likely, only) body and mind, the ability to rotate as a corkscrew like someone with Johnson's physique (he is significantly taller, leaner, and about half my age) will, quite simply, never happen. The day I hit the ball with his power and consistency will occur when Mars turns into a chocolate cupcake. It ain't gonna happen no matter how hard I work. I'm not built like Johnson, and I certainly don't have his physical attributes or his golf skills. That was the swing example this instructor felt would be useful to show me as he tried to improve my golf swing–I was supposed to replicate Dustin Johnson! The instructor went over (in nauseating detail) nearly every aspect of Johnson's swing, from his foot, leg, and arm positions to the massive torque generated by a powerful lower body. I had no option but to simply admire the swing of Johnson and smile back at the completely oblivious teacher. Needless to say, I never came back to have a second lesson with him.

It's obvious to grasp that the physical characteristics we each possess–size, weight, strength, flexibility, etc., will always have a limit. As we all age, more things need tweaking or stretching than they did the year before. I can turn a degree or two less as my flexibility becomes more challenging, and I can see on the golf simulators my ball speed is slowly decreasing. I am who I am, and I must learn to function within those constraints. I think we learn rather quickly (or painfully) about our physical limits as we observe our peers throughout life. Every 10-year-old knows who on his or her baseball team is better than the others. As we apply ourselves to golf, the same rules apply–some individuals are just better at certain things. Mechanically, some of us bend or rotate better; some of us simply can't bend at all due to a previous injury or medical issue. And on and on with each element or part of the golf swing. Ultimately, playing with our limitations becomes a matter of eventual acceptance of what we physically can (or can't) bring to the game.

Most importantly, and more subtle than the physical adaptation and acceptance we all overcome to play the game of golf, is to understand our mental capabilities and limitations as well. This concept can also be called *golf intelligence*: an understanding of a player's reasonable goals and what are reasonable means to achieve those goals. Perhaps this concept is best described as an awareness of *being*–an awareness of *self*. An awareness of self and aligning expectations is a universal struggle. This concept could even be labeled as *the basic human condition.*

It's interesting there are very few endeavors that force us to become so aware of *ourselves.* Perhaps it's because, unlike most sports, one can play golf if one is able to breathe and strike the ball with a club. Similarly, those who are physically handicapped and interested in the game of golf can enjoy playing a round. There are no limits placed on who can play. However, everyone being able to participate creates a situation where the less abled are surrounded by younger, stronger, more talented players. Being on the same course at the same time as the more talented players forces us to see ourselves and our skills more clearly. The key issue to take away here is the players who will enjoy the game the most are those who accept themselves. Most importantly, they do so with an awareness of their limitations. Elementary as it may appear, having golf intelligence–knowing that I am not a Dustin Johnson, a Tiger Woods, or an Arnold Palmer is critical.

We can admire and aspire to emulate those masters of the game, but do so with a sober and reasonable expectation of ourselves and our skill set. No matter how many images someone shows me to try to replicate Johnson's swing, it isn't going to happen. To play, experience, and enjoy almost anything mandates a realistic awareness of self.

# Chapter 9
## *Multitasking*

We all like to think we're good at multitasking and feel emboldened to juggle several 'things' at the same time. In reality, we are all quite bad at multitasking. When doing several things at once, your mind is divided between them, so it's only natural that your mistakes will multiply. According to researchers, multitaskers are terrible at filtering out irrelevant information. Another study showed the symptoms of interrupted work range from psychological to physical. For example, a major downside of multitasking is a feeling of anxiety that plagues people that constantly divide their attention. With multitasking, we are unable to maintain 'flow' states of steady thought or progression–the mind must reset to each task following a shift.

If you ask beginning golfers what they are thinking about before they make a swing, you'll probably reach the same conclusion each time: They have *way* too many thoughts racing through their heads. They are thinking about their posture, grip, backswing, downswing, head position, pelvis rotation, stay down, hit down...the list of thoughts and concerns is overwhelming. There is so much mental activity being exerted in

91

so many directions. As a result, none of those individual focus points are accomplished. Instead of the swing movements occurring as intended, nothing productive happens. The swing appears awkward and flailing–often, the ball will end up dribbling off the tee–if it's hit at all! On the other hand, if you ask an accomplished golfer what he or she is thinking during their swing, the answer is quite the opposite: They may have *one* swing thought...or *none* at all. The advanced players try the opposite of the beginner: They try to keep their minds quiet. In essence, *no multitasking*. With so much to focus on for a proper swing, how can a novice reach a state of mental calm? How do any of us eliminate the noise that runs through our heads almost constantly?

One thing at a time.

Observe an infant who wants to get from point A to point B. He or she doesn't start by running. He doesn't start by walking. In fact, the infant doesn't even start by crawling. The infant will start by squirming around on the floor. The developing brain is learning how to move each body part independently but also in a synchronized manner. At first, the infant's movements are uncoordinated and appear almost random–because they are. The brain is probing its own body by learning its physical limitations...how far limbs will flex, extend, and bend. The infant is learning how much force is required to move itself or each limb against the floor or wall. *Proprioception*: the sense of body position that is perceived both at the conscious and subconscious levels. It encompasses a complex neuro-understanding of the location, movement, and action of parts of the body. Proprioception is the brain 'knowing' where body parts are relative to each other in three-dimensional space. It allows the brain to direct how much force, movement, and joint articulation to use in order to accomplish a particular task or activity. This proprioceptive learning is what is being acquired by the developing brain as the infant is squirming about on the floor. The brain uses every available sensor–vision, haptic feedback, joint position, etc., to find its way in space. But, such complex learning doesn't occur quickly. As we all know, it takes months to acquire the skills to eventually transform the squirming motion into a directional crawl. With additional trials and experience, skills are subsequently acquired to then navigate the world upright. This advanced level of movement also requires the development of strength and motor coordination (cerebellar function) in addition to the proprioceptive requisites. And even once upright, there are stumbles and falls until the complex sequencing of balance and movement are mature in their synchronization. These are extraordinarily complex growth developments that have taken neuromuscular development and evolution eons to evolve.

Multitasking

When starting a new task as complicated as a golf swing, why does the beginner feel he or she should be able to do so without failure? Why do they get so frustrated and so angry at being unable to accomplish the required intricate series of movements? Not only is there complicated neuromuscular integration occurring to swing a club properly, but the timing and tempo of this activity must be sequenced as well. And if that isn't enough, consider the fact most of the golf swing is completed outside the visual field of the golfer. While swinging a golf club, a player can only see down and in front–where his or her head and eyes are directed. The player relies on proprioceptive skills to know where the *moving* clubhead is located in the space *behind* him as the club is swinging and rotating. And that's just to get the club back.

Within milliseconds of reaching the top of the swing (mandating exquisite balance, synchronization, and coordination), the golfer must shift his weight from back to front and *almost* simultaneously allow the quickly moving club to come into direct contact with a 1.68 inch ball at an arm and club shaft distance away. The golfer is doing this while swinging a club he really can't see at a high speed. To add another layer of difficulty, the golfer is trying to swing the club in such a manner that the face of the clubhead strikes the ball squarely without any angular deviation. This entire process must be done with such precision!

If the ball is struck by the club even a few degrees off, the ball will fly 20, 30, or more yards offline. We have all observed learning to crawl was challenging. Perhaps knowing what is involved in swinging a golf club allows us to give ourselves a bit of a break.

The bottom line: Hitting a golf ball as intended is terribly difficult. Expecting to perform this task consistently and as desired at the first, tenth, or thousandth attempt is simply unrealistic. As students of the game (and we are all students at different levels), remember to be kind to yourself. Understand we have limitations of our mental and physical capabilities–despite what our expectations are demanding. Golfers are asking their bodies to perform an extraordinarily difficult task.

Use the capabilities your brain and body have developed over the years. You already have the mandatory 'equipment' and the requisite neuromuscular coordination. But you must stay out of your own way. Work at one thing at a time–build upon it, and then add another, and then another layer of learning. This process of learning, feeling, and experiencing where the club is in space takes repetition and rehearsal. It may take a player years to advance from one stage of playing to the next. To allow your capabilities to work, don't overwhelm yourself with swing thoughts. Just as multitasking doesn't work outside of golf, it will destroy any chance of advancing in this game as well. Limit your swing thoughts and see what happens. Most importantly, be patient with yourself.

# Part III
# The Subconscious Game

# Chapter 10
## *The Subconscious Game: Introduction*

The following chapters explore psychological and neuroscience theories applied to fictional characters for whom the game of golf has elicited intense reactions and deeply personal reverberations. We're not implying that these scenarios or characters represent everyone's golf experience, nor are we suggesting that all golfers facing difficulties need psychotherapy. Obviously, not every frustration with a challenging game reflects deeply rooted psychopathology. In fact, we believe the vast majority of players handle the game with grace and decorum and have little, if any, psychological stress that would require 'professional intervention.' An after-round gathering in which players share a drink and commiserate is affectionately referred to as the '19th hole'. This non-professional intervention is often all that's needed to shore up golfers' spirits.

We have all witnessed or experienced moments during a round of golf that call for a deeper understanding regarding the 'character revealing' aspect of this game. Perhaps these moments reflect the unique circumstances encountered by golfers, unlike other competitive sports. This isolation could stem from golfers being 'on their own,' not part of a team. Unlike most other sports where athletic moves are more automatic and reflexive, in golf, there are long stretches of time between shots–time possibly used to dwell on negativity and failure. The golfer has an inordinate amount of time to think about each shot, many of which may not be what was desired. Perhaps a golfer can feel exposed, alone, and even chagrined as all mistakes are documented on the scorecard. Without other team members to share bad outcomes, the face-saving act of cheating can be testimony to this feeling of exposure for the golfer.

It is in this unforgiving context nearly all of us feel the occasional sting of frustration as we attempt to advance ourselves in the game of golf. Unfortunately, for some golfers, these otherwise natural reactions can become more extreme. As an attempt to analyze the potential root causes of 'poor' behavior on a golf course, we are introducing the reader to 'Gus' and 'Frank.' These two fictional players we have developed will hopefully expose the reader to an insider perspective of what could be responsible for someone's actions and behavior in the game of golf. The deep dive into these characters is an attempt to illustrate, in a magnified way, how we all have a 'past'–a background narrative that shapes our reactions and impacts our living in the present. While Gus and Frank are extreme, their stories serve as a lens to understand human behavior: what motivates and shapes reactions.

The great majority of us are able to maintain and control our behavior–regardless of what adverse or unwanted events occur. Looking into the psychology and etiology of other's perspectives and behavior (Gus or Frank) may help us to be more accepting of our own reactions when we lose our equilibrium. Not every event is extreme; sometimes, something simply rubs us the wrong way. We get upset, and then, eventually, most of us find a means of acceptance and move on. Others have more difficulty with this process. We hope our examples will be useful in helping to understand whatever version of frustration enters our own games (both in golf and life).

We want to move beyond the typical self-help slogans and bromides, which, in our view, promote a simplistic approach with quick fixes–much like the training aids discussed in an earlier chapter. Instead, we are hoping these extreme cases can lend insight and perspective on how difficult and challenging the resolution of problems can be for some. Perhaps it will help us reflect on how we unwittingly bring aspects of ourselves into our own challenging arenas. We hope you find this journey into the subconscious enlightening.

# Chapter 11
## *Magical Thinking*

A day in the life of your average amateur player might begin with his daydreaming about his next round of golf while 'toiling' away at his day job. Our player's name is Gus. Even though Gus has been playing golf for the better part of his life, has taken years of lessons, is an avid reader of *Golf Digest*, and has spent countless hours watching instructional videos, Gus cards an average handicap of 16. As discussed previously, the handicap index is a numeric rating system that represents a golfer's ability to post a score based on their previous playing capability. It also allows golfers of different skill levels to compete fairly against each other. Gus is a dedicated student of the game: he is a member of a privileged local club, plays golf at least twice a week with his regular group, and sneaks out to the practice range whenever he has a spare moment. And, given a predilection for daydreaming, Gus's active imagination sometimes crosses 'over' and can influence his perception of reality. Most of those who are acquainted with Gus would label him an optimist. When playing the game of golf, however, his optimism quickly erodes into an anxious, tentative demeanor. Gus's main issue is that he is unable to bring the important swing 'improvements' from the practice range to the actual course.

On a typical golf day, Gus finishes the $18^{th}$ hole with a double bogey, and his unrealistic dream of shooting a sub-80 round is shattered. *Statistically, only 2-5% of all golfers will break 80 on their scorecard.* Although the likelihood of a 16-index golfer breaking 80 is more plausible than Mars colliding with Jupiter, it is still an unlikely event. Gus looks at his scorecard with a mixture of disgust and shame. The final score is 89, and that's with what is referred to as *equitable stroke control*.

*Equitable stroke control is the maximum number of strokes a golfer can post on a given hole. It's a means to help make handicaps more representative of a player's potential ability, thereby allowing a more reasonable comparison of players' skills. At least, that's the theory. In other words, it is an attempt to limit the true number of strokes a golfer can record for the round to keep his scoring equitable with his skills. Getting more strokes added to one's score will make the handicap go up, which would potentially entitle him to get more of a handicap advantage should that player compete in a golf match or tournament. Hopefully, the game is played fairly, with fair players. But golf is a microcosm of life, and some players will get away with what they can!*

"Damn," Gus states, "had I counted every stroke, I would have been over 90!" The walk to the parking lot is grim. A few waves to fellow players, fake joviality, and then a sad emptiness envelops Gus as he drops his custom-designed clubs and overly expensive accessories into the trunk of his car. He sits behind the wheel feeling tired and achy from the strenuous and unsatisfying 4½ hours of physically and emotionally taxing activity. As Gus sits in the overheated car, his mind shifts to a mental recap of the entire round–each shot reviewed from start to finish. It's a kind of post-traumatic recounting of all his errors committed during the round, along with his recollection of a few bright spots. The occasional good shots help preserve an illusory hope for Gus that *it could have been better.* Gus accepts the reality that he left a lot of strokes out there today. In other words, he didn't play very well.

Armed with this illusion and delusion, Gus goes immediately to his computer and scans *YouTube* titles in golf instruction as soon as he gets home. He is desperately searching for the fix that will finally transform him into the scratch golfer he knows is hiding inside of himself. Again, Gus's imagination is not consistent with reality, as statistically, only 0.5–1.0% of golfers are scratch. Scratch golfers can shoot par or better on any given golf course. Gus is 64 years old and believes there is still time. He reminds himself that with the thousands of dollars he has spent on lessons and videos, he knows more about his golf swing than ever.

"It's not too late!" Gus shouts aloud into the air.

---

There is a term for this type of activity. It's called magical thinking. Magical thinking affects nearly every golfer who fits Gus's profile–and that's a big number. So, what is this magical thinking, and why are golfers especially prone to it?

Magical thinking is a term of art in the psychoanalytic literature. It's a condition that steps in when realistic hope is not achievable. It's the belief that one's ideas, thoughts, actions, or words can influence the course of events in the material world. Magical thinking presumes a causal link between one's inner personal experience and the external physical world.

As described, Gus has fallen prey to magical thinking. When Gus steps onto the practice range, he is ageless, and there is a spring in his step. After all, he had just finished watching a golf video by Russell Heritage (a well-known golf instructor with a large Internet and *YouTube* presence). This jewel of instruction was sent to him by another ageless, magical thinker, and now it was time to put that magical lesson into play. Infused with this latest elixir, Gus brightens up. Surely, he believes that reviewing the video will bring his scores down, and Gus fantasizes about how he will surprise everyone in two weeks when he cruises to win the Club Championship. But the reality for Gus is that the Club Championship came and went. Sadly, Gus finished near the bottom. It was a walk of shame as Gus made his way to the scoring table at the conclusion of the tournament. The club pro accepted Gus's scorecard and, with a shrug, stated, "Better luck next year."

This comment was another cold reminder to Gus that golf can be a cruel endeavor. The game can be very seductive, alluring, and full of promises. But in the end, it can also break your heart. After once again failing to achieve his golf goals, Gus returned home. He opened a beer and sat motionless on the couch. His wife was all too familiar with seeing him in this traumatized, despairing state. A bit fed up with his disposition as well, she chides, "Bad round?"

Gus shrugs and nods. He whispers in a barely audible tone, "Yes, it was miserable."

"Such a shame," the golf widow opines. "Well, don't drink too much." She states  knowing how sullen Gus is feeling.

Gus feels the sting of her comment, and ponders leaving this miserable game of golf. "I'm too old for this shit." He states aloud and twists off the cap of his second beer. After another bottle, Gus reached a conclusion–the same one he had reached many times before–he should quit this torturous game. However, by the next day, he is back in the bubble of magical thinking, and Gus heads over to the practice range. He begins his practice routine and pulls out his 9-iron. And, as has recurred so many times in his golf game, Gus is again inexplicably hitting the ball well. For unknown reasons, his previous bad round is forgotten, and his love for the game is back. His friends see him enjoying himself again, and all is well–for the moment. Such is the magical thinking surrounding the game of golf.

# Chapter 12
## *Gus And Seve*

The recent euphoria that Gus experienced so quickly after nearly dismissing the game previously is a reaction many golfers have. It appears nearly all golfers have a version of Jekyll and Hyde that hovers around their game. What is the cause of this nemesis? Perhaps its explanation is as simple as understanding the problems caused by *second-guessing*.

Reflecting on his play, Gus noticed after a few holes of solid ball striking he would invariably have a *blow-up* hole–one where everything fell apart for no apparent reason. Consequently, he would then resort to feelings of being lost in his swing and helpless to play in the manner he desired. Suddenly, all the old habits were back–the overthinking, the choppy swing, and the bloated scorecard. What was different this time, however, was that instead of his golf round being a long, torturous struggle, it now became one with wild fluctuations. Instead of a steady stream of poor shots, Gus now experienced a series of peaks and valleys in his play. He started to feel as though he had a split personality. Indeed, Gus started to refer to himself as one with this condition.

When Gus was in good golf form, he'd refer to himself as "Seve," after the great Spaniard golfer, Seve Ballesteros, whom Gus always admired. Then, after sliding back into old habits, Gus would shout with dripping self-contempt, "Gus is back!" His playing partners also noticed this volatility–this painful roller coaster of playing ability and attitude. They found dealing with the alternating "Gus or Seve" playing perspective to be quite stressful. So stressful that one of his buddies decided to gently confront Gus at the end of the round.

Jim, his playing partner, said, "You know Gus, this up-and-down demeanor is really wearing thin. Your behavior is becoming a distraction for all of us."

Gus was nonplussed. "What do you mean," he stammered.

Jim replied, "We think you may need professional help. You're a great friend, Gus, but this is hard to watch. This up-and-down behavior can't be good for you...and it's miserable for us to be around."

Gus looked perplexed. With a furrowed brow, he timidly replied, "Professional help? Do you mean a psychiatrist? You think it's that bad?"

"We do," came the somber reply.

Gus walked to the parking lot in shocked disbelief. He thought to himself, *A psychiatrist, for God's sake! What the hell do these guys know? I'm fine...just a little jumpy at times. What on earth? What do I say to Amy when I get home today? She'll probably agree with them. Shit, I'm a mess.*

As Gus predicted, Amy not only agreed with his buddies but enthusiastically supported the idea of Gus getting a psychiatric consultation. Amy asked, "Do you have any idea how miserable you've been since this second self...I think you call him...Seve, has emerged? I don't even know who I'm talking to half the time. And your drinking has increased. You most definitely need help."

Gus replied, "I don't know. I think this has all gotten blown out of proportion. What do those guys know?"

"Gus," Amy replied, "I've lived with you for nearly 30 years. Your friends are right. You've become unstable. I hardly recognize you sometimes. Please consider getting a consultation. Do it for me...for us."

Gus felt a pang of fear. He thought, *is she thinking of leaving me? Do it for us?*

"Ok," he begrudgingly replied, "I'll go...but just for one visit. I'm not so sure I'll trust whatever they say."

"Thanks," Amy replied kindly, knowing this was a huge step for Gus to take. "I love you, and I want you to be well."

"I know, I love you too," Gus replied, but simultaneously felt himself flooded with trepidation. He had a limited understanding of psychoanalysis and what seeing a psychiatrist would entail. Gus pondered his fate and worried, *what am I in for?*

The next day, Gus received a call from the same friend who had confronted him near the parking lot. In a polite tone, Jim had a suggestion. "I've been seeing a shrink myself. I asked him if he could see you or make a recommendation. Because of our close friendship, he thought it best if you saw a colleague of his. The person he is referring you to is Dr. Spielvogel." There was a pause. Gus may not appear to be all that literary, but he recognized the reference to Philip Roth's famous book, *Portnoy's Complaint*. He immediately knew Big Jim was referring to a fictional character.

Gus responded in kind, "Why not Hannibal Lecter?" After laughing off some of the tension, Gus wrote down the name and contact information of the referral. The next day, Gus called for an appointment.

The voice on the other end of the phone was surprisingly unassuming–even disarming. "Hello, this is Paul Johnston. How can I help you?"

Gus stammered, "Uh, Doctor...uh...Paul?"

"Just call me Paul, it's easier," came the unexpected casual reply from Johnston.

Gus was momentarily relieved and then continued. "My name is Gus Sparrow. I was referred to you by a friend of mine, Jim Harris. I was hoping to set up a time to meet."

"Sure," came the easy reply. Paul then stated, "May I ask what prompted your call?"

Gus gave Paul a summary of recent events, culminating with the intervention recommended by his golf buddies and the urging from his wife, Amy. They agreed to meet the following Tuesday. Gus felt strangely relieved as he hung up the phone. That wasn't so bad, he thought to himself. At the same time, it felt a bit surreal. Am I really doing this? Seeing a shrink? Gus shook his head. He felt the familiar sensation of apprehension, similar to how he always felt walking up to the first tee. Gus then had his first therapeutic insight: *I can't control or even predict the outcome. I shouldn't overthink it.*

On the scheduled day of his appointment, Gus drove to Paul's office address and was surprised to find a single-family home with a separate entrance for patients. This was not what he expected or predicted. *Why a home office?* Gus wondered. *Less overhead, I suppose. And an easier commute,* he mused. The office entrance was located at the end of a cobblestone path lined by attractive foliage near the back of the house. It felt secluded and private, which Gus appreciated. Gus felt very self-conscious as he started his *walk of shame* to the entranceway. He wanted to preserve his anonymity.

The rustic wooden door was adorned with a brass nameplate that read: *Dr. Paul Johnston.* No other identifying information was posted. Again, Gus appreciated the nod to his privacy. He gave a gentle knock on the heavy door. There was no answer, so he knocked again...louder this time. With still no answer, Gus decided to turn the door handle. He slowly opened the heavy door, which led into a small but inviting Waiting Area. The room was furnished with two large, brown leather chairs separated by a small round glass table. Strewn on the table were recent issues of *The Atlantic* magazine. As he was a few minutes early, Gus decided to take a seat in one of the chairs and wait. He noticed a Leonardo da Vinci print depicting machinery gears on the wall in front of him. *Hmm,* he thought, *the gears are turn-*

*ing*. On another wall in the small room, Gus noticed a pencil etching of the famous opera star, Luciano Pavarotti.

Gus strained as he looked at the artist's signature in the bottom right corner of the stetching. He realized it was signed by *P. Johnston*. Gus felt a wave of intimidation. *Who is this guy?* He wondered.

The door to the main office then opened precisely at the time of the scheduled appointment. Gus assumed this was his doctor, Paul Johnston. He was short–maybe two inches shorter than Gus, middle-aged, with salt and pepper hair. Paul was casually dressed in khakis and a cream-colored, linen shirt with an open collar. He smiled and extended his hand. "I'm Paul Johnston. Nice to meet you."

Gus shook his hand. "I'm Gus Sparrow." Paul gestured for Gus to enter and asked him to please sit across from him in the simple but comfortable patient chair. The main office appeared homey and seemed appointed to create a quiet, intimate atmosphere. Nothing too garish or distracting was observed. The artwork and furniture seemed to evoke a soft, inviting tone–no sharp edges.

"So, what brings you here?" Paul asked gently.

113

Gus sat more upright in his chair, not at all comfortable where to begin. "To be honest, Paul, I'm not entirely sure. But my golf buddies and my wife, Amy, seem very certain that I need help. I guess I've been moody–up and down, especially on the golf course. I know it's just a game, but it's so important to me. Sometimes, I literally feel I'm fighting for my life. It sounds silly, I know...but the game really has a profound effect on me." Gus stopped for a moment. He suddenly felt anxious about what he just revealed to a complete stranger. Gus came here for answers, not a deep dive into his inner life. And where was this going? Gus pressed Paul to explain what the treatment plan would be.

The dialogue that ensued is an example of how psychotherapy typically proceeds. The invitation to an open exploration of one's private thoughts and feelings can be unsettling.

Paul began, "Well, unlike surgery or other medical disciplines, this process depends on our conversation and how we collaborate in telling your story. There are no tests or x-rays to point to the problem to be fixed. Here we are on a journey together. Like in golf, we're never sure where your thoughts and feelings might go. We must pay attention and follow the next bounce. Sometimes it feels familiar, and other times it can be surprising, even upsetting."

Gus responded, "So there's no plan, no goals, no purpose?" Gus felt annoyed. This was starting to feel like a hole of uncertainty with no end in sight. A journey with no destination–and an expensive one to boot!

Paul was aware of Gus's hesitation. He stated slowly, "I know, it sounds mysterious. But let me ask you a question. What was it like when your friend, Jim, suggested that you consult with me?"

Gus responded, "Well, to be honest, I was shocked...and highly skeptical. I'm not sure why I'm here other than to appease my friends and Amy."

Paul asked, "Your wife, Amy?

Gus answered, "Yes, my wife, Amy."

Paul stated, "And why do you suppose Amy thought this was a good idea?"

There is an adage in the world of psychotherapy, namely, that the work should proceed from surface to depth. Paul could sense Gus's anxiety and guardedness–not an unusual reaction for someone meeting a psychiatrist for the first time. In this first meeting, Paul is mindful of Gus's discomfort and doesn't want to probe too deeply.

Instead, he wants to convey that Gus will set the pace and that he, Paul, will respect Gus's need to feel safe. For now, learning about Gus through Amy, the person closest to Gus, will suffice.

Gus replied, "She thinks I'm unstable, drinking too much... and that I'm developing a split personality."

Paul raised his eyebrows and asked, "A split personality? Can you tell me more about that?"

Gus sheepishly explained his recent adoption of the alter-ego, Seve, as a signifier of his state of mind when his golf game was going well. Paul takes an interest in this self state, not because he has concerns about a split personality, but to the contrary, he sees it as Gus's need to disavow his natural talent as it emerges. Paul believes Gus creates a fictive version of himself, Seve, who gets the credit. But, of course, it begs the question as to why. Why is there a need to disown his emerging success and assign it to an alter-ego? This basic dilemma, which Paul formulated as the core conflict for Gus, framed the ensuing sessions in a fruitful direction.

**Three months later:**

Paul began, "Gus, you describe your father as a domineering figure, the field general, the family patriarch. That he could be frighteningly authoritarian. You also informed me that he was contemptuous of mediocrity."

Gus squirmed in his chair and responded, "Yeah, he could be a real tyrant. And he demanded perfection. Anything less was frowned upon. I could never please him."

Paul interjected, "Unless you were Seve…"

Gus appeared visibly upset and responded, "I don't understand…"

Paul cut him off, "You don't have to understand. It's my job to help you with that."

Paul was unsure about his own response. Was he too quick to reassure Gus? Did he foreclose a more open exploration of Gus's anxious reaction? Paul then realized this was an early manifestation of the holy grail of psychoanalytic work–the transference. Sigmund Freud first coined the term transference to denote the uncanny way a patient begins to experience the analyst as similar to important others in the patient's past, typically one's parents.

At this moment, Gus reacts to Paul as though he is in the presence of his critical father. By not understanding Paul's comment, "unless you were Seve," Gus was reenacting a familiar (and familial) drama. Namely, he felt horrified that Paul would think less of him for not understanding...or not performing as the dutiful patient (son) should. Gus was having a father transference.

Paul inquired, "What happened just now? Why are you upset?"

Gus replied, "I don't know, I just felt stupid."

Paul asked, "Stupid?"

Gus answered quickly, "Yeah, like I just missed a 2-foot putt!"

Paul stated carefully, "That is painful. Can you say more?"

Gus looked down and shook his head, "I feel shame, unshakeable shame. I knew what you said might be important, but I wasn't sure. I didn't understand where you were going, and then I froze."

Paul asked, "You froze?"

Gus said angrily, "Yes, I froze, for God's sake!"

Paul replied, "And you felt alone."

After a long pause, Gus responded quietly, "Yes, alone."

Feeling alone in the presence of others is not an uncommon human experience. It is rooted in the early miscues–the basic fault lines, in one's early relational environment. A tyrannical father, a depressed, unavailable mother, a traumatic loss of a parent or sibling, or a protracted illness–these are just some of the early templates that can be imprinted on one's psyche, along with protective measures, defenses if you will, to keep danger at bay. The danger is the need for connection and recognition by those around us.

### *The session continued:*

Paul said carefully, "You felt alone just now, even though I'm here, sitting right across from you?"

Gus responded angrily, "You? I'm supposed to confide in you?"

Paul began, "well..."

Gus cut him off, "Look, Paul, I didn't come here to be your best bud. I just want to feel better and more in control."

Paul sat back in his chair. He quietly stated to Gus, "But maybe being in control is part of the problem."

Gus was now visibly angry, "You're talking in circles! I thought being in better control  of my emotions was the goal. Now you're adding it to my problem list!"

Paul backed off, "I see your point. Can I try to rephrase that?"

Gus shrugged, looking skeptically at Paul. "Yeah, sure...okay."

Paul stated quietly, "I think controlling and suppressing your feelings were your only options growing up. You've described your mother as withdrawn and depressed, with frequent migraine headaches. Your father is imperious. It's not exactly a warm, welcoming audience for you. So, you adapted. You found other outlets where you could feel recognized and appreciated. You excelled at school, became an engineer, made a good living, and married Amy. So far, so good. But then you got into this challenging game of golf. And it's in this arena that the troubles you left behind are reemerging. In a way, golf has become the theater where you are playing out old dramas. Your feelings are exaggerated, much like they were when you were a kid. And unfortunately, you, again, feel you must go it alone."

Gus suddenly realized where this was all going. He was beginning to appreciate how Paul was disarticulating his troubled past. But this realization was becoming just a bit too painful at this point. Gus needed to stop. It was time to take a break.

# Chapter 13
## *Frank*

Not to use a pun, but let's be frank. We have all met Frank. Frank is the guy we have all begrudgingly been forced to play with–either by assignment in a tournament or, as we occasionally play, as an unfortunate single at another course. Frank is the guy we loathe. Upon meeting Frank, he immediately feels compelled to inform you of a number of things you really don't need or care to hear. Frank first tells you about his handicap (which has no bearing on reality). Unaware of your disinterest in his discussion about himself, Frank then proceeds to tell you what he does for a living (not that you asked), where he was born (not that you even remotely care), and he informs you of his unimaginable successes in life. In a very short time, you have basically reached the conclusion–without even hitting a ball down the fairway, that Frank is just an asshole.

I recently had the opportunity to play with Frank at a member-guest event. These are club events where a member of a golf club invites someone–typically a friend or business associate, to join them in a multi-day tournament. As the member and I made our way to the first hole, we had the pleasure of meeting our upcoming opponents. Brief introductions were made, and believe it or not, the other member's guest was actually named Frank! As I was playing as the guest at this event, I felt compelled to be on my best behavior. If I had met Frank at my own club, I probably would have demonstrated less patience and would have been compelled to excuse myself from the round and just start over with someone else–anyone else. This Frank was the very definition of someone you do not want to play golf with. With his well-over three-hundred-pound mass compacted into a five-and-a-half-foot frame, Frank's physique was not athletic. His large khaki shorts looked more like pants that ended mid-calf. With his huge, bright red shirt, he reminded me of a big tomato.

There were four of us playing together, and on the very first tee box, Frank was upset with two others in our group who were having a conversation while he was teeing off. Okay, I understand that frustration. However, the culprits were at least 30 yards away and whispering in a hushed tone. My hearing is excellent, and I didn't hear a thing. The only way I knew a conversation was occurring was because I saw mouths moving and hands gesturing. I really think the only way to hear what was said in the conversation would have been with an amplified boom microphone. It was really very quiet.

After a pre-shot routine that would mimic The Judge in the film *Caddyshack* (painfully deliberate, time-consuming, and mostly for show), Frank then, finally, wound up and unloaded on his golf ball. He had a terrible swing–it was hard to watch. But even if the tee box were dead silent, it is doubtful anything could have improved the outcome of Frank's duck hook that took his ball far into the woods. I guess Frank just had to blame somebody for his errant hit–anybody but himself. Frank rambled on for the remainder of the hole about how a lack of golf etiquette should not be tolerated. He had to blame his frustration on anyone or anything he could. He managed to shoot a triple bogey on the opening hole. Oddly, however, I noted he only posted a bogey on the scorecard. Despite his knowledge about almost everything in life (I had the opportunity to hear his infinite wisdom during the ensuing 4 hours), it was obvious arithmetic was not in his skillset. I noted this habit of mis-scoring repeatedly throughout the round. Perhaps he could have added numbers properly, but he chose to adjust his scores when it was time to put them down on paper. Whatever the reason, it was obvious Frank simply could not put the correct number on his scorecard according to the standard principles of addition. I guess when one is supreme in their knowledge and perspective of their purpose in the world, mundane tasks such as mathematical addition must also comply with their interpretation of themselves and their expectations. After a few holes, I just let it be. I put what score I thought was correct for him on my scorecard. A debate on each hole was not what I wanted to do. We'll work it out later–or not.

Standing on the next tee box waiting for the fairway to clear, I made a mistake: I don't know if it was out of boredom, but I foolishly asked Frank where he lived. Not that I was all that interested, but I wanted to pass the time. Most people would simply answer that they live in a particular city or state–good enough for the situation. Frank felt the need to tell not only where his primary residence was located–Manhattan (including the address), but also the fact that he also had a home in The Hamptons. Without asking, Frank informed me that he was a member of *several* prestigious golf clubs. I was also made aware of their (significant) initiation costs. In his answer to my foolish question about where he resided, I was also informed about what Frank does for a living and where he does it. Frank explained in agonizing detail that he is the chairman of medical departments at *multiple* hospitals. Oh my. It didn't synapse in Frank's balloon-shaped head that I might know something about medical departments. I just left it as such. At this point, I really had no interest in engaging in any more unnecessary dialogue with Frank. I didn't ask for any of this extraneous information–I foolishly asked Frank where he lived. I asked a simple question, and yet, I became enlightened I was in the presence of someone so very important to the functioning of the planet.

But wait, there's more. After hearing what department he headed, I mentioned a similar department at a hospital near my own home with a national reputation. (It's ranked $3^{rd}$ in the nation). Upon mentioning its name to Frank, he stated, "Yeah...it's okay."

I had run out of patience. I was stunned.

"Just, okay? It's among the finest in the country!" I now exclaimed, having had enough of this blowhole. I then heard a litany of reasons why his esteemed department(s) weren't on the prestigious ranking list. Something about issues with bias and politics mumbled out of his large, fish-like mouth.

When Frank finally ran out of accolades to describe himself, I had to listen to some of his pathetic, sophomoric jokes. It was quickly becoming obvious Frank was not only a terrible golfer with a tendency to lie about his skill level and score, but he was truly just an obnoxious individual. I am not one who is prone to drinking on the golf course. It may well have been the opportune time to start.

Moving along, it was now time to tee off on hole number three...and it was apparent this was going to be a long afternoon. Again, as Frank addressed his ball, he complained about the noise from an electric golf cart moving down another fairway.

I thought the golf cart was well outside of the human hearing range–it wasn't even near us. But with Frank's cat-like reflexes and precise sound-requisites to play golf, it was clearly obvious the barely audible sound emanating from a moving golf cart nearly 100 yards away was the excuse for Frank's ensuing shank.

Frank's reaction to his lack of skill and the resultant shot into a nearby pond was beyond that of a frustrated golfer–it was over-the-top ridiculous. I guess, in the simplest of terms, Frank was a terrible golfer. But not being a good golfer is no excuse to have a complete meltdown on the course. Frank was seething after witnessing another in a long series of bad golf shots. Now, with his guard down, Frank was no longer interested in impressing me with his multiple homes, wealth, and social status. All of Frank's pretense and bravado about himself and his golf game had been exposed for all to witness. Give me a few hours on a golf course with someone, and I will know more about them than I could learn in a year of board meetings. I was wrong about this with Frank–it took just slightly more than three golf holes.

So, how does one deal with a jerk like this? Or, more importantly, how do any of us deal with all the distractions, diversions, traps, and misgivings of our daily lives, let alone while just playing a round of golf? How does one maintain a focused direction while everything in your surroundings is seemingly working against you? It's not easy.

Perhaps the best thing we can do (and what I should have done while in the presence of Frank) is to put on a set of blinders (metaphorically). To be successful with any endeavor, we need to be aware of what is occurring around us. We need to be cognizant of our goals, but just as important, we must be aware of the pitfalls that can impede our ability to achieve those goals. How can a professional golfer properly hit a golf ball despite dozens of cameras being an arm's reach away? Thousands of observers are whispering, chatting, slurping, and eating just yards away, and the pro knows millions are watching every nuance on television. They have learned to tune it all out. And where does that skill come from? I suspect from years of practice.

Perhaps the issue is really understanding how to focus and concentrate. Looking at professional golfers, they work diligently on a refined pre-shot routine. If we worked on this as well, perhaps more of us could then rely on our intensified focused concentration to keep us 'in the game' rather than on everything else. So, maybe the answer to the problem is to *make those routines* our focus. It will surely help us to ignore the distractions from guys like Frank, and perhaps we will eventually learn how to ignore and deflect more things that are beyond our control.

Frank

Our description of Frank relies upon our observation of his behavior and understanding our visceral reactions to these behaviors. Frank is clearly a jerk. We find him self-centered, grandiose, and irritating as hell. His character has been revealed, and it's not pretty. What if we step back from the immediate scene–the painful social encounter with this repugnant character, and ponder what could account for such a noxious presentation? What if we could talk to Frank on a more personal level? One without the pressures of a competitive game and his desperate need to outperform his peers or create the fiction that he has outperformed everyone else. Would he be willing and able to reflect on his repetitive pattern of trying to be more than he is? When all else fails, does he try to convince himself, or even delude himself, that the hard data is wrong and his fantasy wishes are the real deal? What's behind all this bluster? Is there a story that makes some sense of this? Isak Dinesen once said, "All sorrow can be borne if you put them into a story or tell a story about them." But what is Frank's story?

And if we knew more about it, would that help us bear the sorrow of being with him?

These are difficult questions, and they are for another place and another time. On the golf course, we are in no position to engage Frank with psychological explorations–not on the course.

There, we must do our best to ignore the theatrics, the bombast, and the repeated self-serving violations cf rules and decorum. But what if Frank, at the behest of friends, golf partners, and family, agrees to "see someone" about his bad behavior? What might that look like?

Perhaps something like this: Frank's first session with Dr. Johnston, our psychiatrist:

Frank begins, "Doc, I have to say, you have a cozy place here. Small. I don't know, maybe you're just starting out. Maybe you'll get a bigger place someday with corner windows. Who knows?"

Dr. Johnston replies, "Why is it important for you to share those observations of my space?"

Frank answers hesitantly, "I don't know, I'm just being friendly."

Johnston frowned and stated, "That's interesting because it didn't feel friendly. It felt critical, as though you were disappointed that I'm not in a big, fancy, corner office."

Frank responded while appearing mildly tense, "It's not important. I didn't mean anything by it. Look, you're right. I work in a large corner office overlooking Central Park in Manhattan. Hardwood floors, high-end artwork–originals, I might add."

Johnston looked directly at Frank and stated, "That does sound impressive. I have a question, though."

Frank responded, "Shoot."

"It seems very important to you that you are impressive. Why is that?" Johnston asked. "How about just being Frank without all the credentials, the corner office, the money, and the status? Who might that person be?"

With some reluctance, Frank told his story to Dr. Johnston. Apparently, he grew up in a demanding home environment. His mother did not "suffer fools gladly." She was a high-powered attorney in an acclaimed law firm. At the pinnacle of her career, she became the managing partner of this firm and wielded significant influence over the firm's policies and politics–including how younger associates earned a place at the partnership table. She exuded power, and at times, she could be ruthless in asserting that strength. Frank has two older sisters who also became attorneys, but they stayed clear of their mother's path. One became a successful estate attorney; the other a public defender with expertise in family law. Frank's father was a journalist employed by a large city newspaper and known for his advocacy of environmental concerns. Growing up, Frank recalled a well-appointed home, going to private schools, and being attended to by a series of nannies and au pairs. When prompted by Dr. Johnston, Frank described his parents' relationship as transactional but not affectionate. His two older sisters had a bond that excluded him. Neither parent took a strong interest in him. Frank was well nourished, clothed, and managed by the house staff, but he had very few memories of direct interest or curiosity from either parent. Frank continued to describe his childhood experiences and explained, "Mom was always working and seemed stressed and preoccupied when she was at home. Dad was always caught up in the environmental issue du jour." So now we have a bit of a story. Does it change our feelings as we learn about Frank?

Maybe. But on the golf course, he is still a jerk—we still dread playing with him. So, what use is this story? For our purposes, it illustrates, albeit painfully, how golf becomes a theater for our personal biographies. Frank entered his theater on the first tee, and the drama unfolded over the ensuing 18 holes. Frank's need to impress—to outdo his playing partners, to brag relentlessly about real and imagined achievements, and to alter the scorecard, can now be viewed through the lens of a childhood developmental course gone awry. The lack of basic recognition, of feelings of exclusion, isolation, and loneliness now has an explanation. Not having his worth reflected to him by those nearby,

131

Frank desperately looked for ways to prove his significance. The veneer of success and achievement became external salves to his empty self. But in the environment of the golf course, all the unresolved primal dramas get played out. Frank showed us who he really is behind all the bluster.

Witnessing someone's behavior–on or off the course is always reflective of years and layers of experiences, and that individual's associated adaptations to those experiences. Again, not an excuse for obnoxious or undesirable behavior, but trying to understand the origins of how individuals like Frank end up as they do can be useful and challenging. Learning to play (or deal) with difficult individuals can be frustrating and annoying. Recognizing there is very likely a painful personal story behind another's antics may help alleviate some of your reactions. More importantly, it may help you get back to your game and regain your focus. Do your best to ignore their issues. The time will pass.

# Chapter 14
## *Trust*

Trust is defined by Merriam-Webster in the context of a noun as:

a. A firm belief in the character, ability, strength, or truth of someone or something.

b. A person or thing in which confidence is placed.

c. Confident hope.

As it applies to the game of golf, perhaps it is definition 'c' that is most applicable. And yet, by introducing the concept of hope, success in the game involves a perspective of being out of control–of relying upon an unknown force or process to provide the skill to achieve that which is desired. To engage the concept of hope brings the game to a whole new level of the unconscious. Trust in golf mandates the player has, at some point, actually hit the ball as desired, and now, the golfer is relying upon some fundamental level of neurological function to allow that swing sequence to repeat.

But to allow the brain to properly align all the elements of a proper golf swing: small muscles, large muscles, balance, coor-

133

dination, timing, and sequencing–all down to the millisecond, there can be no thinking. There is simply no time to think–only do. And, to perform successfully without thinking, the golfer must rely upon confidence that he or she has done it before.

And doesn't this concept of trust go far beyond the confines of the golf course? To perform almost any activity requires the physical movements of the activity that are already ingrained in our neural network. We already *know* how to perform the task. The key is now determining a means to get out of our way and let the event occur. Does an opera singer have the luxury of thinking about what they need to do during a performance? Or does a race car driver have the time to *think* about what he must do to successfully keep the car on the track while going 225 miles per hour? The obvious answer is *no*. The time allotted for the task does not allow for simultaneous thinking and performing. There is only internal *trust* in what we want or need to do that allows us to actually do it.

*Getting out of our way* does not have a simple explanation. It is something nearly impossible to teach, and yet, it's something we have all learned to do at some point in our lives. We can all *remember* how to ride a bicycle, but do we really remember or think about it when we get on that bike after years of not getting near it? Absolutely not. There is no conscious activity that I perform when I get on a bike and effortlessly maintain my balance—I simply do it. Now, if I tried to focus on all the large and small adjustments I must make to stay balanced and not fall off—I would fall off! I unconsciously trust my brain and body can work synchronously together and maintain my balance so I can ride. The golf swing is no different.

The question one must now ask is how do we gain that all-important trust? Unfortunately, we live in a society that always, and sometimes cruelly, skews our expectations by relentlessly showing us models of perfection (e.g., the Dustin Johnson lesson), along with the myriad of other models of success in every walk of life. In our current social environment, we can never escape all the mirrors of our inferiority. The larger context of an achievement-oriented society cements this way of measuring ourselves. Therefore, you always want or need more.

I will never, ever hit the ball like Johnson. However, one can learn to modulate *expectations* of one's abilities. Until that understanding is reached, the aspiring golfer will forever be frustrated, perhaps angry, and certainly unsatisfied with his or her game. We see this on the golf course all the time. We watch mediocre players (and let's face it, that includes nearly all of us) act as though they should be better at the game than they are. We are all guilty of this. We try to modulate this fundamental competitive part of self, but it isn't easy.

As we look at the game of golf, there is the competitive aspect. After all, it's a game with winners and losers, money and trophies, and comparisons galore. But even if you studiously avoid structured competition–from tournaments down to friendly wagers–it remains a difficult personal journey. Perhaps the challenges of learning the game of golf can be compared to seeking the joy of mastery. When learning to walk, the young child is delighted with discovering this new capacity. The initial stumbles and falls can be quite upsetting, but with persistence, the child becomes proficient, and the walking becomes more natural. At some point, with recent success, the child may erroneously become worry-free with regard to their new skill. Possibly, we will all continue with this *expectation* with any new endeavor we begin. And we believe that if we just persist, we'll get it. But for most of us, this never happens. The stumbles and falls continue despite our best efforts, thus preventing us from truly becoming worry-free. That lack of fear we felt as a child is understood to be a mirage–there will always be some lingering trepidation. Like the young child, we feel mortified that the skill we thought we had mastered suddenly disappears, and we end up falling–stunned and humiliated. And it stays with us. It has been said, "Memory is the special gift of shame." Playing the game of golf requires the player to learn how to have a short memory or figure out a way to forget—so as not to linger on the bad shot.

Confident hope, that is, trust, must rise to the surface, supplanting the shame and stunned humiliation after a fall. Professional golfers excel at this as they have 'learned' how to have short memories. The amateur, who stumbles and falls, tends to have a longer recollection of events. The psychological burden of memory and shame then eclipses the process of regaining confident hope. All of this, of course, emanates from the overall frame of expectations. At some point, whether we like it or not, to advance ourselves, we must come to a realistic appreciation of what we can—or cannot, accomplish. Learning to play within yourself is not easy. You can think of it in terms of personal ambition. However, one's ambitions must match with a realistic understanding of talents and skills. If they don't reconcile, we find ourselves frustrated and, consequently, flailing on and off the golf course.

The grandiose character, Frank, is basically lying to himself because his poor play is such an affront to the ideal self he yearns to be. He lies, he cheats, and he bends reality to hide the glaring discrepancy between his skills and ambitions. The neurotic and depressive character, Gus, struggles to maintain his self-esteem.

The game becomes his psychological nemesis–a "bully trying to humiliate him."

We are all boxers in the ring with a formidable opponent in the game of golf. But does this not mirror our very human struggles off the golf course as well? Our talents and skills may or may not match up with the myriad of challenges we face in our daily lives.

Accepting this uncertainty is never easy. In a live taped interview, Carl Rogers, one of the founders of humanistic psychology, responded to a patient expressing dread of what lies ahead for her. He told her, "Life is risky. There are no sure bets."

How can we ever experience confident hope, our working definition of trust? How do we reach a level of self-confidence or trust that enables us to say, "I know I can do this? The answer is that it's not a linear process. You don't get there through a sequence of lessons or how-to manuals and then graduate with honors in confidence.

Instead, trust or confident hope is a relational, emergent phenomenon. It slowly presents itself through consistent efforts to self-reflect and to gradually accept a more emotionally honest version of ourselves. It requires an openness to engaging and learning from instructors, fellow players, and, yes, even psychotherapists. Trust–in ourselves and others, is simply a very difficult achievement–on the golf course and in our lives.

# Chapter 15
## *Thinking Without Thinking*

How to succeed without thinking or overthinking turns out to be a universal dilemma for athletes of all stripes. Great athletes often refer to "being in the zone" when they are at their best. The "zone" refers to a state of mind that is highly focused and relaxed at the same time. Perhaps it's best described as being fully aware yet not thinking–at least not thinking in a linear, problem-solving mode. An everyday example of this might be signing your name. This is something we all do practically every day, and it is done with full awareness but without micromanagement. You can test this out at home: Sign your name in the usual manner, that is, without devoting attention to each movement of your pen stroke. Now, start your signature with full cognitive attention to each movement and try to perfect your signature. Soon, you'll notice thinking how to manipulate the pen will lead to a choppy result. Your signature will look stilted and unnatural. What happened? You were overthinking it. Instead of allowing the brain's already learned management (established neuropathways) of the movement you wish to accomplish, by actually thinking about the effort, you got in the way of performing it! You had too many pen-stroke thoughts. Similarly, too many swing thoughts are an all-too-common malady for the average golfer like Gus.

Golf is supposed to be a *game* that we *play*. But it seldom feels that way. Experientially, it is more akin to a *discipline* with rules, measurements, penalties, and hierarchies. This hierarchy can be seen by the 'handicapping' of golfers' skills. As previously mentioned, dedicated golfers carry official handicaps–a number that is calculated by a district golf association. The golf handicap is based on the players' recent scores dutifully reported to that association. Gus is short, overweight, and has a handicap of 16. Given that the best players in his club may have handicaps as low as '0' (or even better–but that is a discussion for another time), he obviously is not high up in the hierarchy of golfers at his country club. Certainly, his modest handicap of 16 is not a measure of how much he enjoys the game, how well-liked he is at the club, or his devotion to the game. But...it does arrange a type of pecking order that the players will use. After processing all the insights and perspectives Gus has gained through his sessions with Paul, Gus wanted to try to push all of it aside for a while and work again on the mechanics of his swing. He dragged his clubs and multiple bags of balls to the range for what was surely going to be another repeat of trying to improve his swing.

But this time was different–Gus had an epiphany. He wasn't quite sure if it came from actual experience, a flash of recall from one of the many books, magazines, or videos he had consumed, or whether it was planted into his brain by the so-called 'Gods of Golf.' But the actual source of this sudden onset of wisdom didn't really matter: For the first time, Gus felt something new and exciting!

What was new and exciting? When Gus hit his last ball, he didn't feel *anything*! *That was odd,* he thought. Gus performed his usual pre-shot routine–which typically involved staring at the ball for at least 30 seconds. This alone was responsible for no less than 10 different swing thoughts to enter and exit his mind. Gus then took his usual practice swing. As usual, it felt awkward, uncomfortable, and slightly painful. But then, for reasons unclear to Gus, he shut off his mind and simply swung the club. What happened next was an exceptional experience–which golfers dream about. The ball went sailing high into the air with a trajectory and sound he had never seen or heard ever before from a ball he had struck. Without thinking about his swing, the club struck the ball with a perfect *pfft* sound and without any actual sensation at the moment of impact. The ball flew true. It went straighter and higher than any ball Gus had ever hit. And yet, as Gus would recall, he felt nothing! No strain, no pull, no ache. It was as though his mind, body, and club were one.

Wanting to experiment with his newly found success, Gus decided to repeat everything. He placed another ball on the ground, did his usual pre-shot who-knows-what, and then Gus *found a way* to turn off his brain. Gus swung the club with complete abandonment and without a thought in his head–*Bam!* Another mighty blow! *How can that be?* Gus considered what he just experienced. He had been told a thousand times by his playing partners, his teachers, and, as he recalled, even his wife, *to stop thinking.* This was the first time he applied that 'theory.'

Gus spent the next two hours on the range, trying to repeat himself. He did...and then the magic was gone! Gus suddenly couldn't find it. He did everything he could to try to free his mind while hitting, but the effort of trying to be devoid of thought only created more anxiety about not being able to clear his head. Gus was caught in a loop of thinking about doing something but not actually being able to *do it*. The intense effort to focus–on not focusing, was getting in the way of success. At first frustrated, Gus eventually resigned himself to the realization he touched on something critically important: The ability to do it is there; he just needs to learn how to bring it out. Perhaps this was one of the most useful lessons he ever had–and he did it on his own. Gus is well aware of his mediocre golf scores and is ambivalent about his golf skills. Consequently, he always approached each round with apprehension and anxiety. Not only was this *not* a means to enjoy the game, but it also caused him to focus so much on what he needed to do to strike the ball properly, that he always got in his own way. As he would go through his pre-shot routine on the first tee, Gus would typically feel his muscles tighten...anxiety mounting...and he would have an ominous anticipation of failure. Gus was always so caught up in his effort not to fail he couldn't recall moments of freedom and effortlessness on the range. Where did that go? Perhaps, he thought, next time will be different. Gus was determined to try to replicate the experience on the range.

The following day, Gus was apprehensive about his ability to repeat his experience on the practice range. But he prepared himself and went out to the first tee. Gus teed up his ball and thought about keeping his head steady, his hands quiet, his lower body leading, the upper body following, turning but not swaying, clearing his hips, and *covering the ball* as he swung through the impact area. The resulting swing looked and felt like a choppy signature–mechanical and forced. Instead of rehearsing his thoughts with his practice swing and then just repeating the motion, Gus overthought the process. He did not allow or *trust* he could repeat the swing motion he experienced on the range just a day earlier.

On the next shot, Gus swings–the ball flies weakly to the right and settles in the rough. This sets up a difficult third shot. Gus shakes his head, feeling a stab of shame and despair. He walks to his ball, knowing he will be first to hit his 3rd shot as all three playing partners outdrove him by at least 60 yards. According to the rules of golf, the player whose ball lies farthest from the hole plays first–a dubious honor that is bestowed on Gus all too often. Gus regroups, and an interesting thing happens. Out of his despair, he conceded he simply could not get better at the game. At this point, his emotions are a mixture of frustration, embarrassment, and anger. Gus is so despondent with himself that he tells himself the hell with it. And that is exactly the moment when he shuts off his thinking. Instead, he swung at the ball without any preconceived concern for an outcome–Gus absolutely stripes it down the fairway! The epiphany is recalled, and Gus shouts to himself, "It's in me. I just need to get out of the way!" With his thoughts quieted Gus was able to perform as desired. Indeed, with his effortless swing, the ball flew off the clubface with minimal effort.

Obviously, mindless swinging will not always lead to a desired outcome. The very complicated synchronization of the components of the golf swing must be learned and relearned. The neural pathways involved must become patterned in our brain. This will only occur with focused repetition. Some will learn it better, and some sooner. Some will be able to ingrain those pathways if the game is learned at a particular age—generally, younger is better than older. But, perhaps, in a sense, when we speak about not thinking, we are really stating the mechanics of the golf swing must be learned so well they are transitioned from a conscious part of our brain to the unconscious part–when the swing movements and synchronization become as natural as walking...or writing one's name. How to get to the point of not thinking is one of the most challenging parts of any endeavor. But it's a point we must reach if we are to succeed. Just as in the writing exercise described, try doing the same with your next golf swing: See what happens when you just let it go.

# Chapter 16
## *Confidence*

Confidence has multiple definitions, descriptions, and expectations. For instance, as defined by Merriam-Webster, confidence is a state of mind or a manner marked by easy coolness and freedom from uncertainty, diffidence, or embarrassment. The Oxford Dictionary states that confidence is defined as feeling sure about your own ability to do things and be successful. Etymologically, confidence comes from Latin, specifically the noun *confidentia* from the verb "to confide." The Latin prefix con-, a variant of com-, usually means with, together, or in combination, but here, it is an intensive prefix meaning *completely*; the verb *fidere* means *to trust.*

We use this singular word–confidence, to describe such a complex, almost perverse sense of being: To have complete trust. We throw this word around so easily, yet its meaning is so very difficult to explain, let alone achieve. Is there any one of us who has complete trust? I trust in the laws of physics. There are a series of laws of physics, such as the Laws of Thermodynamics, Newton's Laws of Motion, the Law of Universal Gravitation, and so on. But to have complete trust in oneself? I honestly

147

don't know of anyone who possesses that trait...and if they did, would I even want to be around them? Probably not. The concept appears so enticing, I think, perhaps, I'd like just a single slice. Yes, please–just a thin, little slice. And if I had that slice, what could I do with it? How would a small amount of confidence allow me to achieve my goals–and not let me get in my own way? And at the same time, how would I not upset everyone else with this newly acquired force in my arsenal for achievement in life? But then, by definition, if I had such confidence, I would be beyond embarrassed or concerned about what others thought about my having it. Yet, at the same time, I don't know if I could handle the consequences of not caring. I need others–I need to know my presence is desired and valued and that I can effectively make a difference. I need friends and family. A display of too much confidence could push everyone away. This is an endless circle of decision and indecision–of cause and effect, creating more problems than solutions. What does one do?

I don't believe there is a best answer to this conundrum. We all want to have what confidence can bring, and yet to have it is typically associated with a touch of arrogance, a lack of concern, or even an absence of consideration for the perspective of others. To be confident implies you may not have the answer, but you don't really care if you don't. You don't care how others perceive you...because you are confident in yourself. Is this really what we want?

So, yes. Just a thin, small slice will do–just enough to get the job done. Or will it? By even questioning myself, I'm obviously demonstrating my lack of confidence! And here we go again. In describing what we want, there is a constant circle of unsureness–definitely not demonstrating the definition I'm trying to achieve. Is there a universal answer to address this dilemma? No. Perhaps we must each choose our priorities and hope they align within acceptable parameters with those we care about or feel the need to be with.

After all, we are social beings. The need for vital connections with others is fundamental. Infant research demonstrates relational-seeking right from the start. Social integration is integral to us as a species and necessary, if not always achieved, in society writ large. Developing confidence becomes a delicate interplay of seeking recognition and getting realistic feedback from important others. For instance, we learn as kids that not everything we do is worthy of praise–we are all flawed. And yet, in the constant back and forth with our social environment, we learn about the world and, hopefully, about our particular talents and skills that gradually become recognized and recognizable to us. We develop some 'confidence' in our talents and skills as we become integrated members of our society. Of course, this is the ideal blueprint. There is no need to explain the myriad of ways it can go awry.

But let's get back to an arena, a society within a society, where this quality of confidence is tested to its limits: the game of golf. We all remember our initiation into this society. Fledgling golf toddlers, flailing away, feeling ambitious, and typically having meager, inconsistent results. Most of us went through a long period of confidence-draining interaction with this game. Let's face it: most of us still do. But then we inevitably start sharing our plight. We confide in a friend, a parent, or an instructor. In other words, we seek relational sustenance to boost our skills and, yes, our confidence that we have those skills. This is typically a long, arduous struggle for most. But the payoff can be a more accurate appraisal of ourselves as golfers and, more importantly, a more thorough understanding of our capabilities. If all this support goes reasonably well, and admittedly, there are many ways it can go badly, this at least gives us a chance to move forward in our understanding of the game and of ourselves. Keep in mind that golf can be merciless. Your bad shots and bloated scores are there for everyone to see. Confidence is aspirational, and it is unrealistic to think it will always be there; it gets lost and recovered. However, the recovery requires a willingness to observe and reflect on this elusive state of mind as it is part of our personal and social makeup. Most often, we do need others' help to get back up, much like a toddler needs an attentive parent to help after a fall.

Perhaps the true definition of confidence is more challenging than any dictionary has yet been able to describe. We can read and appreciate the literal definition, but its experiential application is much more delicate and problematic. Exercising confidence is not the same as defining it. Perhaps it all comes down to knowing what you need to do, learning the means that will enable you to do it, and then accomplishing your goals without injury or prejudice to others. Now, that's confidence–knowing your goals and then achieving them.

# Chapter 17

## *Gus and Seve Part 2: "Golf as Theater"*

The phrase "golf as theater" really hit home for Gus. He recalled how when driving to the golf course, he would typically be rehearsing his performance or, when driving home, critiquing it much like a theater critic. These previews and reviews could be all-consuming, sometimes dispiriting as well. Frantically, Gus might call his teaching pro to set up an emergency lesson or check the *YouTube* channel to find out how to fix a recent swing flaw he identified.

During his psychotherapy sessions, Paul would refer to these critiques as internal commentaries colored by Gus's earliest critics, his parents and siblings. Being the youngest of three children, Gus felt small and inferior. He was nearly a decade younger than the two older siblings, prompting the existential question, was he even wanted? Gus wept for the first time in therapy when he recalled his siblings sharing exciting stories at the dinner table that had nothing to do with him.

In one of his last books, Philip Roth muses about our "ridiculous quest for significance." We carry this quest from our earliest interactions with the world around us. We strive to achieve a sense of mastery of our environment, with how we function bodily, socially, and psychologically. Importantly, we also strive to control how we manage painful experiences.

Golf is casually referred to as a game, implying a playful, pleasurable form of recreation. But for Gus, as well as so many of us who take the game so seriously, it's hardly a simple form of play. It's a complex activity that can stir a myriad of reactions, from well-controlled sportsmanlike conduct to throwing clubs and regressing into an infantile tantrum.

How does this happen? How does a responsible adult with a career, family, and social network suddenly regress into a red-in-the-face, hair-on-fire primitive creature throwing a fit while heaving his 7-iron? All because he hit an errant golf shot?

Really? Yes, really. Our golfer hit a bad shot–but that is simply the manifest story.

Let's return to the consulting room as Gus shamefully recalls his "bad behavior" on the course:

Gus began, "I was doing fine up until the 16th hole. My game was holding up, and I felt hopeful that I could salvage a round in the low 80s, maybe even a sub-80 round. I just had to avoid a big miss...just play steady and not push for too much glory.

Then it happened. I watched helplessly as my drive sliced into the fescue–a lost ball. For the scorecard, this mandated a loss of stroke and distance."

*According to the rules of golf, if a player hits a ball out of bounds or loses it (the player has three minutes to search for a ball before it becomes lost), the player must go back to the spot of the previous stroke to replay the shot. In essence, the golfer loses a stroke and needs to still play the distance. (There are some newer amendments to this rule to help speed up the course of play, but the essence of being penalized for the errant shot remains).*

Paul was less familiar with the detailed rules of the game. He asked, "Then what happened?"

Gus replied without emotion, "I snapped."

Paul appeared puzzled, "You snapped. What does that mean?"

Gus replied, "It means I had a meltdown. "I yelled, "Fuck me!" and threw my driver. I mean, I really threw it into the air straight out into the weeds." It was then quiet for a long moment. Gus looked at the floor, averting Paul's gaze.

Paul quietly asked, "Then what?"

Gus replied, "I went to pick up the club and apologized to the guys, but I knew they were very tired of me and my outbursts. It wasn't long after that incident that Jim suggested I see you."

Paul sat back in his chair, looked at his notes, and then continued. "When you say you snapped, can you talk more about that? Try to drop back into that moment...tell me what you were feeling inside."

Gus stared at Paul and then, after a lengthy pause, replied, "Hatred."

Paul paused on that response for a moment...and then asked, "Hatred of whom, of what?"

Gus answered quietly, "Of them...of everyone watching while I felt like a total fool."

"Then what happened...what did you feel?" Paul probed carefully, knowing this was an important moment in their therapy.

Gus replied, "I felt raw anger, totally unfiltered."

Paul asked, "And then you threw the club. Did that internal, agitated state then change?"

Gus was now visibly tense. He responded, "Yes, somehow throwing the club felt like revenge. Like I got back at them–the guys watching me flail, the game itself...which felt like a bully trying to humiliate me. I wasn't going to take it anymore."

Paul asked, "And afterward?"

Gus replied, "Afterwards...driving home, I keep asking myself, What the hell was that? Frankly, I was perplexed and embarrassed. Throwing the club seemed ridiculous, but at the same time, it felt...almost necessary."

What we see here is that angry reactions on the golf course are often multidetermined based on one's developmental history and temperament. Although Gus appears to be an immature hothead at first glance, a closer look reveals his deeper intrapsychic conflicts that find their way into his golfing persona. There are clues to these conflicts in his sessions with Paul. The profound disappointment following his golf shot into the fescue reverberates with earlier experiences of feeling inferior to his more successful siblings. Instead of sharing their success stories, he feels excluded, a loser. Gus feels a wave of self-hatred ("fuck me!"), and instead of mastery, he experienced a profound loss of self-regulation ("I felt like a fool").

In this fragile state of self, the world appears persecutory–the other players and the game itself are experienced as bullies trying to humiliate Gus. He then throws his club, a misguided attempt to reassert his dignity ("it felt almost necessary").

The forgoing has been an explanatory framework for the unfortunate and distracting eruptions of anger that we see (and experience) so often in what is commonly referred to as "just a game." It's an explanation with the hope of humanizing those moments that are so painful to experience and to witness.

In the moments that followed, Paul tried to humanize what Gus was depicting as monstrous behavior after a bad shot. Paul stated, "It was your cri de Coeur."

Gus asked, "My what?"

Paul answered, "Your cry from the heart. You were on the cusp of a great score only to stumble at a critical moment. You then cried out in sorrow after your failed attempt. It's perhaps something like the slalom racer who falls near the end of what could have been a record-setting run."

Gus nodded in agreement and then said, "Sure, but it's golf! I'm not supposed to throw my clubs. It's different. Everyone feels bad for the skier who falls. With me, everyone just sees me as a bad sport or, worse, a crybaby."

Paul responded, "Very true. But my point is that you don't allow yourself that moment of sorrow. You go straight to your bad performance and humiliation, and then you project these feelings onto your buddies and onto the game itself. You jump right over your sorrow into persecution. Then you throw your club in protest. As though you are announcing, "I am not a loser!"

Gus replied, "Yeah, and then I just make it worse. Now I'm an out-of-control loser."

Paul listened carefully to what Gus just stated. "What happened just now?"

Gus said, "I feel sorrow."

Paul replied quickly, "Yes, and that's real! You're no longer in the theater where everything is exaggerated, and you're fighting the demons from your past."

Gus said slowly, "Yeah, I'm beginning to see that. But I'm aware of other things as well...that I'm older, that my body just can't respond the way it used to. But I can't accept it! I keep expecting more from myself. Every now and then, it happens...the stars align, and I hit the ball as well as I've ever hit it. A booming drive, or a crisp 8-iron that lands softly on the green, or a 10-foot putt that finds the cup. But I can't sustain it. Why not? I know more about my golf swing than I've ever known. I'm a student of the game. I'm devoted!"

Paul replies…"but you're older."

Gus pauses. He knows Paul is right. Hell, he just said the same thing a moment ago. But isn't that the 'human condition,' he wonders? Aren't we all in some form of denial about aging, declining, and ultimately dying? So, what's the point? Why go on?

Gus responds, "So why go on? Why keep struggling? I know I'll never get to the mountaintop. So, what's the point?"

Paul looks curiously at Gus, "Well, with that logic, why even begin?"

Gus answers, "In the beginning, there's hope…"

Paul asks, "Hope for what?"

Gus responds, "I don't know…perfection? Eternal bliss? A sub-par round? Maybe not to feel so tormented?"

Paul considers what he just heard and responds, "The torment, the sorrow, these are feelings evoked by your "failed attempts" on the golf course, but they refer to the failed attempts to elicit your mother's love or to find your voice at the family dinner table. It seems that your pain is misplaced. In a way, you are expecting your golf game to heal old wounds, but then you are devastated when that doesn't happen. Your expectations are not only inflated but your golf intelligence is diminished. You start reacting like the traumatized child who feels rejected, unwanted, and unloved. Golf as theater, remember?"

It's been said many activities can build character; golf reveals character. We can think of character as a collection of predispositions. Character, then, refers to our tendencies to react to external events, but more importantly, how we define those reactions internally, i.e., what personal meanings get attached. All this mental processing occurs in milliseconds. The end result is an outward expression of this process–an emotional display. This is all we really 'see'.

Gus throws his club, and this now becomes an external event for the other players and for Gus himself. One player puts his arm around Gus, trying to console him, while another feels disturbed and looks away. The 4th member of the group feels angry, fed up, and tells Gus he needs to see a psychiatrist. No one, including Gus, considers this moment a cr- de Coeur.

Even though most of us, if not all, can identify with the sentiment–namely, the sorrow of the failed attempt. This behavior, as it occurs in the context of the social rules-bound game of golf, is considered, at best, unacceptable and, at worst, a psychiatric disorder.

And in our opinion, this is as it should be.

The foregoing analysis should be confined to the consulting room and not acted out on the golf course. Gus's friend, Jim, finally set an appropriate limit, and Gus benefitted much like an acting-out child might benefit when appropriate limits are set on his or her infantile behavior. The overriding principle here is self-regulation. Golf can reveal cracks in this developmental capacity that previously were not evident, even for the otherwise 'well-adjusted' individual who ventures into the deep waters of this amazingly complex activity–this game of golf.

# Chapter 18
## *Gus and Seve – Conclusion*

Gus had now been in therapy with Paul Johnston for over a year. Although his golf game, or rather his reaction to his golf game, was the main precipitant for seeking help, Gus could now see *golf as theater,* which was precisely what had been happening. He had become a 'method actor' of his own personal drama, and the golf course was his stage. Gus acted out all his 'issues' until his buddies finally had had enough. With careful and painstaking analysis, he and Paul were able to examine those agonizing moments when the *game* became a bully trying to humiliate him–much like his older siblings who mocked him for being small and inexperienced. Being able to observe and gain a perspective on this in therapy helped Gus see this tendency as just a part of himself–a very young and vulnerable person. But Gus understood these issues didn't define him–it wasn't all of who he was. Gus now understood this part of himself with Paul's assistance and guidance. And, with some compassion applied to the understanding of why things occurred, Gus now knew the proper perspective was to just let it be–these issues didn't have to take over. The adult part of him could emerge more fully. Yes, golf can be upsetting, frustrating, even agonizing. But that is a visceral reaction that can be tolerated. It does not need to become a full-scale theatrical production.

**The Final Session:** Gus began, "I want to thank you for helping me deal with all my issues. Understanding what was happening is not what I expected."

Paul sat back in his chair and inquired, "What surprised you?"

Gus replied, "The situation with me is not so black and white...It's not Jekyll or Hyde...I can be both...we coexist. I had to learn how to live together with this other part of me." Gus paused and looked down at his feet. Looking back up, he met Paul's gaze and stated, "In the beginning, I really thought you were a quack!" They both laughed. Gus continued, "No, really...it was as though you were just another bully out to humiliate me."

Paul reflected on what Gus just remarked, "The bully was really inside of you, though, wasn't it? It was a defense your mind set up, ready to pounce on any perceived weakness."

Gus perked up, "That's right! I'm my own worst enemy... that's what I had to realize. You gave me the space and the time to slow down and start to recognize that."

Paul replied, "All I think you needed me for was to be the compassionate listener, which you gradually started to identify with. Now you are better able to soothe yourself–as Gus–with all his foibles. You no longer need to be rescued by Seve."

Gus smiled and answered, "That's funny…I haven't referred to myself that way for quite a while now. Seve feels like a childhood imaginary friend that has faded away. Good work, Doc!"

Paul smiled back, "You know it was a joint effort. You did a lot of hard work, and it paid off."

With that, Gus and Seve parted ways. And Gus was able to end therapy with Paul. Was he feeling cured? No. More resilient? Yes. In terms of his golf game, Gus noticed a definite sense of relief. Instead of the old pattern of approaching every shot with fear, he felt more relaxed and capable. The final score was no longer a marker of Gus's self-worth. Not that he didn't care… he cared as much as he always had. But now Gus could allow an element of curiosity to be a part of his reaction to an errant shot. Instead of a theater production, golf was now a work in progress. An activity that could be experienced as a game–something to struggle with, to play with. Golf was now perceived as something that was challenging but not persecutory. Gus was finally having some fun playing golf–he would never have thought that was possible just a year ago.

# Chapter 19
## *Gus and Seve, Postscript*

There is a term used in contemporary neuroscience called the *Default Mode Network* (DMN). It refers to the brain's tendency to reduce uncertainty–to 'smooth out' all the unpredictable stimuli and create a kind of 'handshake' between the brain and the world. Unfortunately, this default network can sometimes get rigidified, leading to repetitive patterns of thinking and behavior that are often detrimental, i.e., habitual self-doubt, anticipatory fears, being too hard on oneself, etc. In sum, a self-defeating pattern can get lodged in the psyche–in the DMN, and foster a negative attitude that becomes resistant to change.

So, how does this relate to Gus? The whole point of golf as theater is that early developmental experience tends to get laid down as well-worn pathways of thinking and feeling. This includes our typical ways of reacting to stress, frustration, and even our successes. These patterns become woven together over time into what we commonly refer to as someone's character. When we refer to someone's character, we are talking about the predictability of their reactions to a variety of stimuli. Character is resistant to change as behavioral patterns become habitual and automatic. The DMN is the neurological substrate for this kind of un-thinking, un-reflective reaction pattern. There is little to no time between stimulus and response. As a consequence of the DMN reaction, there is no time to reflect, ponder, or consider one's multitude of reactions—it's automatic.

When Gus hits a bad shot, he does not think; rather, he just reacts. There is no pause between stimulus (bad performance) and response (anger and humiliation). One important aspect of Gus's progression in psychotherapy was learning to effectively insert a 'pause' between stimulus and response. This allowed Gus to reflect on the meaning of a bad shot, i.e., how the DMN immediately puts it in the category of failure or inadequacy and how that meaning belongs to a very early developed pathway, namely humiliation and rage. The psychotherapy process helped Gus reflect more and react less. We want to emphasize the word 'process' here. In a way, Gus had to learn how to think, not simply what to think. This is yet another version of holding on and letting go. Most purveyors of golf wisdom give clear and convincing advice on what golfers should let go of. They will adamantly tell someone any of a variety of phrases: "Don't dwell on it!" "Have a short memory!" "Perfect is the enemy of the good!" These are all good pieces of advice, and there are hundreds more. However, the problem with these concepts is they quickly get lodged in the DMN as another rigid prohibition. It becomes the psychological equivalent of a training aid–the promise of a quick fix without lasting results. In this context, holding on refers to one's willingness to think and reflect on particular dysfunctional reactions–to own and try to understand them in order to then let them go.

As Gus became more acquainted–and accepting–of his long history with his internal bullies and how this was played out in the theater of his golf game, he was able to gradually carve out new pathways of thinking and feeling about the inevitable misfortunes on the golf course. Could he have done this on his own? With a good friend? With a good golf coach? Very likely, yes. However, the healing environment of an attentive therapist and the creation of a safe space to reflect proved to be vital in achieving a new level of integration and peace.

After nearly a whole season away, Gus rejoined his old group, now as an alternate. A new recruit replaced him as a regular.

"Welcome back, Gus. How've you been?" asked Jim.

Gus replied, somewhat impishly, "I've been on a sabbatical."

The new player, Darryl, asked quizzically, "Was it some kind of expedition? Where did you go?"

Gus looked at Darryl, "I traveled far and wide to great heights and great depths."

Somewhat perplexed, Darryl responded, "Well, I hope you had fun."

Gus laughed, "Yeah, it's been a blast. But now I'm ready to play." Indeed, playfulness was a hard-won achievement from his "expedition." Gus played the round in an outwardly uneventful manner. Importantly, he was noticeably more relaxed and less reactive.

At one point, Jim put his arm around Gus and said, "It's so good to have you back."

Gus looked at him, paused, and finally nodded, "It's good to be here!"

Gus's walk to the parking lot and ride home were routine—without the previous habit of negatively ruminating about his game. When he walked through the door at home, Amy asked him sheepishly, "...well?"

Gus replied, smiling, "Piece of cake. It's just a game, you know."

# Part IV
# Concluding Perspectives

# Chapter 20
## *Finding The 'Wa'*

'Wa' is a significant philosophical concept of Japanese culture. I am not Japanese; I don't profess to have a detailed understanding of Japanese history or culture, nor am I an expert on Japanese literature. However, the concept of 'wa' is something I was exposed to while visiting and exploring Japan. I've endeavored to understand its meaning and applications. From what I grasp, 'wa' is a simple, mono-syllabic term reflecting an extraordinarily complicated concept: harmony. It is a term used in Japanese culture to describe harmony in being, harmony in attitude, and harmony in action. Harmony: a state of balance among forces–compatibility.

I have worked hard to learn the game of golf–not simply as a series of sequential movements and physical maneuvers to propel a small ball through the air, over the ground, and into a hole. By looking at the game with a wide prism, I have gained the understanding that golf is a microcosm of the game of life. It is also apparent to me that understanding the game of golf as a form of 'wa' is paramount to understanding its very nature. Only after appreciating the game through this vantage point was I able to undertake and apply myself to it more effectively.

Golf as a microcosm of life? That might sound arrogantly poetic for a game of hitting a small ball around in the grass. Perhaps this statement is just a shade too over-the-top. Or is it? Let me explain something I have identified while playing golf. This is something I alluded to earlier, and I believe it warrants reiteration: give me four hours with someone on a golf course, and I will tell you more about their personality, their ability to deal with untoward situations, their temperament, and honesty than I could glean from spending months with the same individual outside of this arena. Playing golf with someone reveals more about their nature than anything they say about themselves or what you've heard from others. The game of golf reveals how someone deals with obstacles and hazards or is stuck in the deep rough–literally and figuratively. Golf will show how humble one is when good fortune comes their way or how insensitive someone can be when a paucity of luck finds his fellow players. As noted, golf will reveal someone's temperament–how they handle both good and bad outcomes. In essence, the game will tell you practically everything you need to know about someone.

I was once approached by an accountant who wanted to be hired to manage my business account. He called multiple times and explained how he could find ways to save my practice thousands of dollars in taxes and expenses. Apparently, this person had worked with a relative of a friend, so he was already partially vetted–or so he implied. I was intrigued with what the accountant was selling, and I thought it would be reasonable to meet with him to hear his recommendations. During one of these phone calls, I found out he loved the game of golf, so we made plans for a golf *meeting*. I thought this would be a tremendous way to meet the man behind the promised financial gains. With a mutual interest in golf and, more importantly, my finances, we set up a tee time.

The two of us met on the driving range at his private club. After perfunctory "hellos" and a brief warm-up, we planned how we would discuss his financial recommendations; we would play the front nine without any business 'talk', and then finish up the round engaged in a financial discussion. Although I typically walk while playing a course, the accountant insisted we ride in a golf cart. I became his passenger as the green fees were on him, and I was his guest. So far, so good. The plan for the afternoon was reasonable–what I witnessed during the round was not.

Although the accountant considered himself an intermediate player–one who had obviously taken lessons to learn how to robotically set up to his ball, take his stance, and strike the golf

173

ball in the manner as instructed, he still needed more lessons to learn how to hit the ball with consistency and distance. In other words, he was like the great majority of players—he possessed some golf skills and desperately wanted to improve upon those that were lacking. But the difference between wanting those skills and having them are far from synonymous. Taking lessons and 'knowing' how it should be done is a far cry from being able to actually execute those skills. Sometimes, as I have witnessed, the line between one's desire and ability can be a bit fuzzy.

As we started on the very first tee, my playing partner proceeded to discuss his perspectives on spending, saving, and investing. Somehow, the previous plan to just play golf and enjoy the day for the front nine went out the window. With no option but to listen, I diligently obliged him. He talked the talk, and I listened like a young student—painfully aware of my shortcomings when it came to financial matters. The accountant was in his wheelhouse when it came to knowing tax issues. What he was saying did make sense. However, his golf game was another story.

After a few lucky starting holes for him, the accountant's true golf game revealed itself—it usually does. A couple of duffs here and there, and then frequently topped balls, started to visit his game. He was hitting everything just a few inches above the ground. Soon, the dreaded *shanks* appeared in his game. This is bad. For the uninitiated, the golf shank is one of the most dreaded shots a golfer can make. It's so bad we con't even want to say the word out loud. Basically, a shank occurs when, instead of the club face striking the golf ball during the downswing, the ball is struck by the hosel (where the shaft connects to the club head). When this occurs, the ball typically shoots wide right (for a right-handed player), and it is a completely uncontrollable shot. Not only does it look awful, but it feels worse. Nobody seems to fully understand why this mishit suddenly appears in someone's golf swing, but often, it's difficult to get rid of. Suffice it to say, it's a bad thing to happen to a golfer–let alone when someone is trying to impress you on how well they play the game. Once this occurred for the accountant, everything else seemed to go wrong for him. He missed multiple short putts, and his chipping was on the brink of disaster. As much as I was doing my best to be pleasant through a painful afternoon of observing his suffering, I knew I was there to hear about his financial recommendations. I empathized and gave him my most consolatory words as he self-destructed.

Okay, no problem–I get it. The game is tough, and we all have ebbs and flows during a round. I really wasn't playing with him to be impressed with his golf game, but rather to share this mutual interest while discussing my tax issues. But as we were sharing a golf cart, I had the opportunity to look at the scorecard when he left to find one of his lost balls. I was aghast. Did he really just record a bogey when he shot an eight (a triple-bogey)? I thought back on several of the holes we had just played and recalled how he managed to three-putt most of them. I vaguely recalled a four-putt that occurred somewhere as well. Didn't he also lose three balls on the last four holes? His golf game was terrible, but how did he score just a bogey on each of those holes? His recorded scores had no resemblance to reality.

What I appreciated at this point was that he may be experienced as a knowledgeable accountant, but he lacked a particular skill I thought was mandated for that profession: *honesty.* I'm quite sure he knew *how* to add–after all, we were just dealing with single-digit numbers–even though, to his credit, some of them were prime. But *consistently,* he recorded scores that had no bearing on what he actually shot. His artificial scores reflected a more significant issue for me. I knew at this point there was no way I would allow him near my books. If I couldn't trust him to keep an accurate golf score, there was not a chance in hell he would be my practice accountant. The golf game revealed who he truly was–and I don't think it was his inability to perform simple arithmetic. Importantly, I understood he wanted to be better than he was. All golfers want the same. The accountant couldn't acknowledge he was a mediocre golfer–this is nothing shameful. I wasn't his competition nor a regular playing companion. I was someone trying to learn about him and what he could help me with professionally. What I experienced was a person who wanted to be somebody else, and the only way he could do it was to basically lie on his scorecard. But what bothered me the most was that while we sat and had a drink postround, he told me about his golf score! It didn't occur to him I could actually see it on the cart, or I could even count his shots myself! It was as though he was in complete denial of his actual game. At the end of the round, I thanked him and bid my adieu.

The accountant couldn't accept his golf game's reality. There was no sense of 'wa'. There was no harmony and no balance between what he aspired for and what he actually was. I prefer an accountant who can keep his score and my books with accuracy. Most importantly, I value someone who has an honest perspective of themselves and their behavior.

Another event occurred with a different golfing 'buddy.' This time, it wasn't his inability to count correctly–his golf scores reflected that he could do that fairly and well into the triple digits. No, playing golf with this individual revealed to me his insecurities. He once explained to me in detail how anxious he became over each shot. At first, I shrugged off his excuse as typical first-hole jitters. But after just playing one round with him, I was convinced he truly had an absolute fear of failure–

which in turn led to more failure. The never-ending cycle of a self-proclaimed, self-fulfilling prophecy of defeat was his modus operandi. I realized he lived his life in fear. Again, the golf game quickly revealed personality traits that were not obvious in other settings. This golfer lacked confidence. But more importantly, he lacked an understanding of himself and how to find the right path to personal success. He lacked a sense of 'wa,' a perspective of balance.

Just as the game helps us to see through the camouflage of those we play with, perhaps golf's greatest attributes lie with it providing a means for the player to self-identify and allow self-reflection. This assumes, of course, that the player is able to open him or herself up to self-assessment. This has nothing to do with the realization that someone is a good putter or a good driver of the ball—that information is self-evident. The game provides the opportunity for the player—stripped of all pretense and talk, to *feel* how he or she reacts to what just occurred.

---

I line up my shot, perform my pre-shot routine, and strike the ball. What I envisioned before the swing was a 150-yard high draw with the ball landing softly on the green and rolling toward the pin. What I experienced was the ground being struck well before the ball and my 'fat' shot limping along the ground a few dozen yards or so before being stopped by the deep rough. Now, the issue that needs to be addressed is how I react to that event. I have multiple options: I could sigh heavily, think about what just transpired, and make a note to readjust whatever I need to improve next time. I could let out an expletive and toss my club farther than I just hit the ball. I could blame the golf cart that was 100 yards away and didn't stop to wait for my shot. The excuses are endless. However, the actual explanation for what just occurred is that a swing mistake was made. It's up to me, the player, to decide how I wish to try to correct what just happened. Similarly, it's up to me to decide and determine if I can find my sense of balance, my sense of 'wa', and get back into the game.

We all experience frustration. The key is to address the root cause of our errors and resolve it. And, as in many other aspects of our lives, if we can try to focus on the causation and not the outcome, moving forward will most likely be more productive. We can't change what has happened, but we can try to modify how we respond to it. Golf sheds light on us to see our own actions and reactions to failure and disappointment. Whether or not we are honest with ourselves will become evident...if not to ourselves, then to those we play with. The game of golf is constantly asking and pushing us to seek harmony within ourselves. The game doesn't lie, although sometimes its players do. Playing the game as it was intended and having a realistic understanding of your skills and capabilities is paramount. The game reveals who someone is. Seek to find a sense of balance and harmony in your game–both on and off the course.

# Chapter 21
## *True Golf Envy*

**E**nvy: a feeling of resentful longing aroused by someone else's possessions, qualities, or luck. A desire to have a quality, possession, or other desirable attribute belonging to someone else.

I think everyone has experienced envy. Perhaps it started at the age of two or three at one of my first playgroups. Although I can't exactly recall the precise details, I'm sure some other kid with a runny nose had something I wanted–to either hold, eat, or just put into my mouth. As I grew older, whenever someone in my age group got a new toy, ball, or anything shiny, I simply wanted it. Most of the time, it really didn't matter if I actually needed whatever the object of my desire was–I simply wanted it. Therefore, it became something that I became obsessed with. Looking back, that obsession only lasted until the next shiny object appeared in my view.

As we golfers progress in life, more expensive toys appear on our horizons, and we lust after them. Hopefully, we gain financial independence, and most of us can now afford these things. I can't think of a single person I play golf with who doesn't look at or at least consider purchasing the latest in gadgets, clubs, or apparel. We absolutely love golf paraphernalia. Just the thought of having the opportunity to walk into a golf superstore–needing something or not, is exciting. The golf superstore is really the grown-up version of a toy store. Many of us who are addicted to the game–who pay steep club dues and go on frequent golf trips are secret shopaholics. We do our best to keep this habit under wraps, but despite our efforts, the failure to hide this aspect of our personalities is painfully obvious to everyone else. There are probably only a few golfers roaming around who can demonstrate a modicum of restraint with regard to upgrading their apparel or equipment. Very few of us can separate in our preoccupied brain the ability to balance wanting golf stuff versus needing golf stuff. Unfortunately, for many of us, it's like quicksand–the more you step into it, the faster you begin to sink. And most of us have all stepped waist-deep into it! I suspect having envy is, perhaps, a natural consequence of being with others and seeing what they have and then believing, or maybe convincing ourselves, those things are what we need.

But True Golf Envy (TGE), I believe, is a different animal altogether. This isn't the same as wanting a new club or a pair of the latest shoes. No. TGE is a dangerous, insidious aspect of the game we wish to avoid, like the plague or maybe even leprosy. TGE is well beyond the 'stuff' of golf. TGE is something we all want to avoid at all costs. It's painful; it's agonizing. Indeed, for many golfers, TGE is impossible to eliminate from their lives, and consequently, its effects invade other aspects of their worlds. Some may seek professional help in dealing with TGE.

Let's begin our description of TGE by first describing something that is much simpler and more understandable: Simple Golf Envy (SGE). SGE is the predicament created by not having what another player is athletically capable of doing in the game. SGE is best defined as the desire to have the physical attributes and ability to hit the ball with distance and control, as performed by those you aspire to play like. But it's more insidious brother, TGE, is not just the desire to play better. It's a situation brimming with jealousy, frustration, and anger. Resentment takes over acceptable, productive behavior. TGE occurs when one is so trapped in trying to excel (in golf) that the unfortunate individual is unable to meet reasonable expectations for themselves. The affected player's competitiveness has gotten out of control and has become self-destructive.

We compare ourselves to others; how else would we know where we fit into whatever hierarchy we are evaluating? But TGE occurs when that comparison leads to such misery from the game we simply can't function or behave properly. Ineffective management of this comparison to play better results in ugly behavior–throwing clubs, sarcasm, nastiness. In a word,

183

the player is simply miserable. We all want the ability to play to our expected levels of capability. Indeed, we crave to do so. But when we don't accomplish our goals, TGE can take over, making the experience of failure even more potent and damaging.

Many championship players have described how they 'move on' when adversity occurs on the course. For instance, Tiger Woods has been quoted saying that he had a 10-step rule. He would allow himself to think about an errant shot for only 10 steps–that the undesired shot was over, and nothing would ever change that fact. After a moment of reflection regarding what went wrong, it was then time to move on to the next shot. He focused and prepared himself for what lay ahead, not for what was unchangeable in the past.

It takes considerable skill to be able to move a ball up, down, left, or right. It takes skill to putt the ball where and how desired. And, of course, it takes skill to smack the ball far down the middle of a fairway. However, to have the ability not to be affected when the ball doesn't move across the green or in the air as desired is truly an advanced state of being. Having the ability to hold on and move on is what avoiding TGE is all about.

And isn't it so in life? We can't change the past. We can't modify what previously occurred in investments, work, or our interpersonal relationships. We can ruminate forever about things that happened yesterday–and such wasted activity won't change a thing. Such ineffectual behavior consumes an inordinate amount of time and energy in so many of us. It takes us out of the present and into the past, where we can't change a single thing. Of course, we can study and learn from our mistakes–and we should. But then it's time to move on. Decide on what to do or how to act, and then do it. Obviously, most events in our lives will require more than '10 steps' to process and separate ourselves from their outcome. Some situations in our lives may take years to overcome. However, understanding and managing what has occurred must be accomplished at some point to move forward. Ultimately, the consequences of that event must be accepted before you can go onto the next step, process, or plan–or golf shot. Perhaps it's easier said than done, but nonetheless, to get to the other side of the pain or anguish, expectations must be reasoned and accepted.

TGE–the inability to effectively accept a mistake or the failure to achieve an expected level of accomplishment. Focus your energy to learn what it is you are aiming for, and then make a plan to go forward. If your efforts are rewarded by achieving your goal, well, wonderful. But if not, then figure it out or seek help to figure it out. And then, move on.

# Chapter 22
## *The Uneven Lie*

We need to state the obvious. Life is not fair. It's unfair that some are born with attributes enabling success or achievement, while others lack the capacity or capability. It isn't fair some are brought into the world with privilege and wealth while others must work exceedingly hard just to keep their heads above water. We have no say regarding which family, decade, or century we exist. Many of us expectantly wonder what it will be like in 20, 30, or 100 years. Yet, how many of us could have survived if we had to fight in the civil war or were born under tyranny? How many of us could successfully uproot our families during times of oppression or war? We live in an extraordinary era where many of us can pursue our desires and strive for what we want.

In many ways, golf is no different. We may hit the ball better than our opponent, but our ball may land hundreds of yards away in the grass, in a depression in the ground, or perhaps in the exact location where a previous player hit his ball, leaving a barren area in the grass. That barren spot is referred to as a divot hole. A divot is the result of a piece of turf gouged out with a golf club in making a stroke. And no, it isn't fair that my well-struck ball ends up in a divot hole. Rules are rules, and the golf rules state the ball must be played where it lies–no exceptions are made. Hitting out of a divot hole can be challenging, particularly if it is deep or the ground underneath is hard and packed. Sometimes, just getting the face of the club down to the ball sitting in the middle of a divot hole is difficult. The surrounding tall grass will make the ball appear below the grass surface, causing the golfer to try to hit his or her ball out of a small pit. Many times, the subsequent shot will not come out as intended: it may be topped or spin in an awkward direction. The distance the ball flies can be difficult to predict. And...you did nothing wrong to have to deal with this lack of good fortune to end up in this situation.

And, as in life, a golf course fairway is rarely a predictable surface. It will have areas that are completely flat and others concave or convex. There will be slight hills and valleys; some areas are growing well, and others are not. The mowing of the grass over certain areas will be consistent, whereas more difficult areas to access will be variable in their maintenance. A ball that ends up in deep, unmown grass can be nearly impossible to hit out. Sometimes, areas of sand (bunkers) will be hard and flat, leaving the ball sitting up. Other sand hazards will be soft and deep, resulting in a ball landing there that is half-covered and quite challenging to hit.

Different golf courses have different types of grass. Some grass species thrive better in certain climates. For instance, variations in temperature, rainfall, elevation, or the amount of daily sunlight can determine which type of grass grows best in a particular location. Each grass type behaves differently when a golf club moves through it. For instance, golf courses played in harsher climates tend to be composed of very hearty species of grass. The grass in these regions is mostly fescue–tough blades that resist being uprooted by a club. Divots are difficult to make, so consequently, it can be hard to get a club through and under the ball. In the deep south, Bermuda is a frequently encountered grass type. This grass is soft but tightly 'knit.' Hitting a ball out of this grass type is akin to hitting out of Velcro—the grass grips the ball. Players need to have experience with these different grass types in order to play successfully on them. As expected, some players will have grown up and learned how to play on these variable surfaces, whereas visiting players–perhaps in a tournament–will have less exposure and knowledge of what to do and how.

One of the more challenging surfaces to hit a golf ball is when it is on an uneven lie. The ball is sitting on the ground above or below the player's feet. This can also occur with other variables. Maybe the ball is below the player's feet...and is on a sidehill slope. The ways the ball can land, roll, and then need to be struck again en route to the hole on the green are nearly endless. A well-hit ball landing on an uneven lie...perhaps accompanied by being in a divot, perhaps surrounded by grass a player is less familiar with...perhaps, perhaps. Challenges are everywhere!

The environment above the ground can also have a significant impact on one's game. Is the day sunny, or is it raining? Is the wind mild, or is it howling? I have played on days (particularly in Scotland or Ireland) when heavy rain is being blown by the wind so hard it isn't landing on your head–the rain is hitting you in your ear. Umbrellas are useless with strong gusts, so we simply trudge onward wearing layers for warmth and water repellency. Yet, the golfer's score is recorded on those days just like it is on the calm ones. There have been some recent changes made to our handicapping system to take into consideration significantly bad weather. However, on the majority of difficult playing days, inclement weather doesn't seem to be considered in this algorithm. Stroke adjustments are rarely implemented, perhaps not even in a hurricane.

The golfer must adjust to the weather, the grass differences, the undulations, and defects in the fairways–those intended and those not. The golfer must learn the nuances of the greens he or she is putting on and be able to determine which factors in nature will cause the ball to roll one way or another. The golfer must use the best of his skills to manage a course that is designed to protect itself from being too easy. A course is trying to decipher which of the players is best at this game.

And isn't it the same off the course as well? The pitfalls, the enticements, the misrepresentations, and the inability to see what lies ahead afflict us all. We must learn to tolerate what we can't control and do our very best to weather the storms. We all experience uneven lies and events that are not fair or even deserved. But what are our choices? Take your favorite club and do your very best to get out of the divot hole.

# Chapter 23

### ...There

Do we ever reach *there?*

One of the basic goals every golfer attempts to fulfill throughout his or her golfing career is to improve. It doesn't really matter where you are starting from in your game; we all want to get better. Whether you are a scratch golfer, a single-digit handicapper, or someone who plays to an index in the mid-twenties, we all want to squeeze that extra little bit out of ourselves to get *there*.

Perhaps the actual number of shots of improvement is less important than the relative number of strokes. This means that for the higher index player, the ability to shave 5-10 strokes off their round can be significant. For the scratch player, improving by just one or two shots can be momentous. And, as each player practices diligently, he or she becomes consumed with what they need to do to reach that next level of play.

This raises the question: What is *there?* And do we ever truly attain it?

...There

*There* is a very rare place to be. No matter how well we play, we all want to get better–whether this is truly within our reality or simply a fantasy–every golfer feels they can and must improve–we all want to get there. The 17-handicapped player wants to break 90, and the low single-indexed player feels he or she should always shoot below 80. The scratch player, who wants to break par, is aiming to shoot below 72. So, there is no defined there. *There* is a level of play that lives within the hopes and aspirations of each player. It is never the same for any of us, and it may be unreachable for most.

For some, being *there* may not be an actual score at all–it may simply be the fact that they outplayed their opponent. Maybe the actual number of shots improved matters less than the relative number of strokes. For instance, thumping another club member may be the ultimate goal for the season. So, my 112 strokes, which beat your 120, maybe my there. Consequently, the definition of *there* becomes even more conceptual and difficult to define. *There,* and all that it entails–both actually and perceptually, can be an elusive abstraction of our expectations.

Do we ever reach *there?* And are any of us so confident in ourselves or in our game that we can ever stand on the podium and say, now I am *there?* Even the greatest golfers of history were constantly tweaking their games–searching for that one extra

192

morsel of improvement in their quest for there. Tiger Woods, arguably one of the greatest players to have ever played the game, is constantly working to find a better way to play and score–to hit more consistently and with greater distance and accuracy. Did he ever find it? He would probably say "no". Ben Hogan, another golf great, has been quoted as saying he "hoped he could hit two good shots in a round exactly as he intended." Seriously? I would gladly take all his unacceptable shots. Yet, the Sunday afternoon duffer who just thumped his playing partner 112 to 120 would probably triumphantly open the door to his home after the round and announce to whoever was there to listen how he "found it"! I have a close friend who once proudly explained to me that he "owned" a course. Upon my query as to how he reached that conclusion, he informed me that he broke shooting 100 at that course. He was as proud as a peacock. Personally, I would hide that score from everyone, yet to him, it was his pinnacle of scoring. He felt he was there. The score wasn't as impressive as his perspective of accomplishment. Perhaps we should all learn from him and take pride in even our smallest achievements.

Is *there* merely a concept that soothes our need for hope, keeping us engaged in this challenging game of golf? Perhaps it is just a fantasy. Do we ever reach our desired destination? As much as we strive for it–the endless hours of practice, the miles driven, and the dollars spent on equipment and lessons, achieving it and getting there appear to be circular goals with no real beginning or endpoint. Trying to just touch these unreachable points of achievement is, perhaps, the catalyst that motivates us to keep at it. For those who play the game of golf, whether you are 8 or 88, you will constantly be on the circular path to get *there*. Maybe it's the refusal to accept that you've ever truly reached that mark that keeps you coming back for more.

Is life outside of the fairways and practice range any different? Are we not in a constant struggle each day to seek and find *there? There* is defined in the 'real world' as a certain level of success in life. Isn't *there* really reflective of a level of self-peace and balance? Most importantly, aren't we really expending our daily efforts to experience joy and satisfaction through successful behavior and action? Perhaps only with that experience can we truly say that we are *there*.

So, is it actually possible that a golfer, as in life, can find it in the game? As circular as the efforts may appear, one could argue that, indeed, one can. Perhaps it's a matter of allowing yourself to accept your accomplishments and enjoy the process. Maybe we need to stop focusing on an end-point–a score, an outcome, and simply work at trying to get better–the *there* will present itself.

# Chapter 24
## *Where Do We Go From Here?*

This book has been an exploration and analysis of one of the world's most challenging sporting endeavors. Golf is a game that began centuries ago. A game that began with a carved wooden stick is now played with graphite and steel alloy shafts and titanium and ceramic club heads. Modern advancements include digital videography and computer algorithms used for detailed analysis of player swings and ball trajectory. The technological advancements have been truly astonishing, as we are now at a point where the overseeing golf associations have recently introduced plans to limit how far the golf ball will travel. Biomedical engineering and medicine now offer deeper insights into human physiology and biomechanics, optimizing a golfer's ability to strike the ball. Professional golfers are hitting the ball beyond the confines of our golf courses. Circa 1900, a typical elite golfer could drive the ball 160-200 yards. A drive exceeding 220 yards was considered exceptional. Recreational golfers at the time drove the ball on average 100-150 yards. Today, we are seeing professional golfers stripe the ball over 350 yards with their drivers. The human body hasn't changed in those years, but our understanding of how to train and swing with maximum efficiency using modern equipment has obviously evolved.

However, what hasn't changed is our human emotional frailties. Our anxieties and fears, our needs and wants, are still the same as when, six centuries ago, some fellas with bent sticks decided to hit a ball into a hole and make it a game. What were their expectations...and were they as focused on success in the game as we are today?

Given our nearly 24/7 accessibility to either watch, play, travel, or play on an artificial simulator, our obsession with the game is constantly reinforced. We watch the professionals play, which may give some unrealistic expectations–they make it look so very easy. Despite the unfair comparison, many aspire to replicate professional skills, especially when they seem effortless.

Expectations aside, what many of us have not mastered is the ability to control our emotions such that they work with us and not against us. And, from a broader perspective, outside of the tee boxes, fairways, and greens, how does one manage to hold on and then let go? How does the emotional and mental discipline required to properly swing a golf club and play the game similarly apply to living a productive, enjoyable life? Or perhaps the corollary should be asked–how does stability in life apply to the game of golf? Is there really a difference?

*Holding on and letting go* in a broad sense refers to the ability to regulate oneself–in particular, one's internal emotional reactions. This is different than suppressing reactions or simply "behaving oneself." It has more to do with self-knowledge and self-compassion, enabling a self-soothing capacity for the inevitable ups and downs throughout a round of golf or, more importantly, in our daily lives.

In terms of mechanics, the golf swing involves rhythm and tempo, much like other athletic sequences. Muscle groups contract and release–we hold on and let go, hopefully with good rhythm and tempo. But the mechanics we need to apply to play this game go far beyond golf. We must learn how to use our mechanics, literally and figuratively, to achieve any success.

There is a dialectic of forces–mental and physical–that must be coordinated to create a coherent composition. This applies to everything we undertake. The game of golf mirrors the game of life. Both are comprised of moments of joy and agony, failure and success–often juxtaposed. Navigating the interplay and tension between these contrasting experiences, both emotional and physical, is what we refer to as holding on and letting go.

Let's go play a round. Experience it, savor it, feel it. Golf is truly a wonderful game. But, more importantly, let's embrace what we have and what we can do.

Let's step onto the course and let the game unfold around us. Experience each swing and each moment of connection between club and ball. Golf is more than just a game; it's an experience that teaches us about patience, resilience, and gives us an opportunity to reflect upon ourselves. But let's not confine our appreciation to the fairways alone. Beyond the boundaries of the golf course, let's celebrate the chance to pursue our passions and life's joys.

So, as we embark on this round of golf, let's do so by reveling in the camaraderie, the challenge, and the experience of just 'being'. Enjoy every swing and every step along the way.

# Acknowledgments

Writing a book about golf–a game that has existed for centuries, is not something that is performed without significant consideration of its storied history. A topic as diverse and complicated as the game of golf was challenging to review as there are so many aspects to consider. Describing the nuances of how to play the game–its rules, procedures, how to hold a golf club and strike a ball, could and does fill bookshelves. We addressed some of these issues to provide context to the book. However, getting inside a golfer's mind and examining why we behave and perform the way we do while golfing was our objective.

Our task required an understanding of the game of golf, and more importantly, it mandated a review of human thinking, reasoning, and perspective. Such understanding came not only from on-course observations but also from over 60 years of combined medical practice as physicians. Professionally, we have had numerous opportunities to witness how people behave–when they are well and, unfortunately, when they are not. We have seen patients, as a psychiatrist and as a surgeon, away from their normal environments–often unsure, exposed, and many times anxious about unknown outcomes and circumstances. These experiences, as well as an ability to observe individuals–both on and off the golf course, gave us the inspiration to write this book about a game we love. We hope you found it interesting, informative, entertaining, and, most importantly, useful.

Our many thanks are extended to the golf professionals who have tried to improve our lives by improving our games. We would like to acknowledge and thank our pre-publication readers who shared their time and insights with us–to let us know what we got right and what we missed. We are hopeful after reading our perspectives and observations, you will enjoy this marvelous game even more.

# About the Authors

## Michael J. Young, MD

Dr. Michael J. Young is a faculty member at The University of Illinois Chicago (UIC) College of Medicine in the Departments of Urology and Biomedical Engineering. At UIC, he is the Director of the Division of Urology Innovation and Technology, and functions as a Medical Advisor at the UIC Innovation Center. Currently, he is pursuing the development of new surgical instruments and medical devices, as well as teaching medical and biomedical engineering students at the Chicago campus. Dr. Young holds patents on various medical devices. Prior to joining the faculty of UIC, Dr. Young practiced urological surgery in private practice for nearly 30 years.

Dr. Young previously authored The Illness of Medicine, a book discussing the current status of our healthcare issues and his experiences as a practicing urological surgeon. He has also written a trilogy of medical mystery novels that highlight our vulnerabilities within the medical environment (Consequence of Murder, Net of Deception, and To Cure or Kill). In his free time, Dr. Young enjoys traveling and photography and, of course, is an avid, evolving golfer.

www.michaeljyoungmd.com

# John L. Perri, MD

John L Perri, MD, is a faculty member of the Chicago Psychoanalytic Institute, where he is a supervising psychoanalyst. He teaches and supervises clinicians in training and provides frequent consultation to experienced therapists and analysts in the field. He also maintains a full-time private practice in psychiatry and psychoanalysis. Although his early training was largely in the classical tradition of Freudian psychoanalysis, Dr. Perri now practices by incorporating more contemporary theoretical models that emphasize the here-and-now relationship, such as Intersubjectivity and Field Theory.

Dr. Perri has a lifelong fascination and active involvement in the game of golf. Over the years, the psychological struggles peculiar to the students of this game became yet another avocation. He counts himself as one of these struggling students.

Dr. Perri's other avocation is the world of enology, especially the old-world fine wines. In his private life, Dr. Perri cites his marriage and his daughter as singular achievements.